UNDERSTANDING YOUR LIFE PURPOSE TRIANGLE

Michelle Da Silva

Copyright © 2016 by Michelle Da Silva

All rights reserved. This book or any portion thereof may not be reproduced or used in any manner whatsoever without the express written permission of the publisher except for the use of brief quotations in a book review or scholarly journal.

ISBN: 978-1-3999-6195-0

ACKNOWLEDGEMENTS

To God, my family, children, friends, challengers, the Angels, Spirit Guides, and all the wonderful, confusing experiences: I would not have learnt if I did not have the good and the bad. I am blessed to be at a point where I can share all of my learning. Because of this, I am truly grateful and give thanks to everyone who has contributed to my life in any way, negatively or positively.

And to my five angels, Martin, Ivy, Tyler, Piper, and Roxie, thank you for your continued support and belief. I am truly blessed to share my life with you.

CONTENT

ACKNOWLEDGEMENTS 3
INTRODUCTION 6
PART I 14
HAPPINESS IS A CHOICE 14
Chapter 1 How Do You Choose to Live Your Life? 15
Chapter 2 Life is Not as Hard As It Seems 25
Chapter 3 Self-Worth and Belief 31
Chapter 4 Your Evolved Mental Maturity 41

PART II THE KEYS TO CHANGE 46
Chapter 5 We Need to Self-Reflect 47
Chapter 6 Becoming the Observer 52
Chapter 7 Remember to Always Be Thankful 61

PART III   THE PROCESS 66
Chapter 8 From the Very Beginning 67
Chapter 9 School and Society Create Beliefs 77
Chapter 10 Learning from Parenting 87
Chapter 11 Self-Identifying Thoughts 96
Chapter 12 Conditioned Expectations 104

Chapter 13 Social Media and the Consumers Market 110

Chapter 14 Understanding Fear 116

Chapter 15 Offenders of Hurt and When We Offend 125

Chapter 16 Can You Ever Experience True Love? 134

Chapter 17 Substitutions and Habits 141

Chapter 18 Comfort Zones 151

Chapter 19 Time and the Quick-Fix Mindset 158

Chapter 20 Understanding Energy 166

PART IV YOUR PURPOSE 175

Chapter 21 Your Purpose Is to Find Your Authentic Self 176

Chapter 22 Become Your Own Miracle 182

GLOSSARY 185

ABOUT THE AUTHOR 187

Introduction

There comes a moment in life when your eyes are opened. But before this, it is as if you have been walking around in the dark. I remember experiencing this feeling of how everything became so clear and simple. Why had I not seen this before? How had I been living for so many years in this way?

I am describing when you finally realise you are having a human experience on this earth. It is the moment when you know that you do not have to live your life with hate, resentment and blame, that we are all connected, and that we are all on this journey together. It is when you understand acceptance and return love even when others have hurt you. It is the moment you realise that people in your past were only able to do what they could and they tried their very best, and you offer them and yourself forgiveness and love.

My moment came for me after I went through an emotionally painful experience. Life became confusing and frustrating because I couldn't understand why things were the way they were. Situations ended that I did not see ending. Plans did not go according to how I thought they were supposed to go. Feelings of disappointment and doubt were regular experiences.

I found myself in a hole that I couldn't find a way out of. Everything that normally worked for me didn't anymore. No matter how much encouragement I received from others to get out of that dark place, it felt like I just couldn't do it. Each day felt like I could only crawl.

Eventually, I did manage to get out of that hole. It was when I decided that was not who I was, and things needed to change. My eyes finally opened when I was able to recognize some of the behaviours I had been exhibiting for so many years and the reasons for them.

I had to take charge and make a choice. I had to put in the effort, and I did.

And I did this by accepting what life presented and reflecting on my behaviour and what needed changing. Later in life, things became even clearer, making me look at life in a different way.

The beautiful thing about life is that there is no right or wrong. Every decision we make is not going to lead to disaster or make us bad people, but it will ultimately bring us to a place of understanding. Boy, there have been times when I felt lost and couldn't see the bigger picture, but looking back, whatever I experienced all made perfect sense.

The Routine

My alarm goes off, and I hit the snooze button. I always do this at least twice before finally getting up. I immediately reach for my phone and go about my normal Web-surf of the news, Instagram, Facebook,

Twitter, emails, and the weather. This is pretty much my morning routine before even getting out of bed.

There I am, looking at other people's social media profiles, never interacting with them, only comparing and judging their lives. Next, I look at mostly terrifying news stories and end by checking my bank balance and sadly thinking, Will I ever have enough money?

I could start every morning looking forward to a new, wonderfully exciting day, another opportunity to work towards my dreams and goals, and to living each moment fully and with purpose, happiness, and meaning. But do I live my life meaningfully, pursuing what I have always imagined myself doing—living my best life?

Probably not, and what's worse, I take for granted, like so many of us, that I have all the time in the world to figure things out. So, I put things off, telling myself I will start tomorrow. Then I just go ahead and spend more time with my head down, looking at the phone and sharing a reality of what's in other people's profiles, instead of waking up and looking out at this amazing world and creating my own amazing profile.

How About You?

Does this sound familiar? Have you found yourself doing these exact same things? You might not necessarily wake up this way, but do you find yourself looking at everyone else's life and wishing yours could be like theirs? Have you reached a point where you feel stuck and have just accepted it because you can't seem to push forward, thanks to too many doubts and insecurities? Or could it be that you just don't know how?

I have a question for you. Suppose at day's end you learned that it had been your last day? Would you honestly be content with everything that you did today and have done up to this point in your life? Would you be feeling regret, guilt, and sadness over everything you never did? Can you say you lived your life in a way that would ensure people would always remember you as you would want them to? I am pretty sure that if someone had told you this morning that today would be your last on earth, you would have said and done things very differently.

Many of us want to do so much but don't know how to get what we want. Some people fail at it, some succeed, and some will always be on the verge of it yet never achieve their dreams. Some of us give up on our goals because they feel so out of reach. Or could we be allowing fear to govern our lives?

All of us experience fear and anxiety in one way or another. I certainly have. Take, for example, writing this book. It took me a long time before I finally decided to put pen to paper. I hoped that by sharing what I had experienced and learned, I would help others better themselves, get through a difficult situation, or offer them a new perspective. I knew that it was something I had to do, so writing this book was a major goal.

Still, even though I completed *Understanding Your Life Purpose Triangle* in 2016, I left it for about six years and did absolutely nothing with it. My book, alongside my goal, just sat on a shelf. Wasn't I ready, or didn't I believe in myself? Was it fear of rejection, or did I think I wasn't good enough to write a book because, surely, I'm not a writer?

Old Messages

Like me, so many of us have dreams and goals that we'd like to achieve, but we don't pursue them because of doubts, fears, or lack of confidence. We all grow up with preconceived ideas about what we are good at and what we think we need to stick with even if we don't like it. Some of us believe we can't pursue our dreams in certain areas because we didn't do well in school. We may have been told we weren't good enough or smart enough to achieve in life, but this way of thinking cannot be further from the truth. Because, sometimes, the very thing we think we can't do, is the thing we should do.

We weren't given an 'adulting manual' when we turned 18. Nor were we given a 'life dictionary' to guide us and the meaning of life's difficulties and lessons. Yet here we all are—once innocent children, now adults—taking on responsibility and challenges, usually with no hows, dos, or don'ts in handling them. *Understanding Your*

Life Purpose Triangle could be that manual about adulting for you.

When I had my moment, initially, I wanted to shout it from the rooftops and tell everyone how easy things could be. All anyone needs to do is accept what happened in the past and what is in the present for what they are. It's no one's fault. We have the power within to do this and always have had it.

Sometimes I did share this message, but others didn't get what I was trying to say. Because if people aren't ready to hear this yet, they won't. So I didn't impose what I had come to understand on others. If someone was open, I had no problem discussing these concepts with them, which is how this book came about. Since then, I have continued to self-reflect and soul search. This process led me to become a professional life coach.

Insight

This book offers insight and understanding about why things may be happening in your life.

We are searching for answers, desperately wanting someone to tell us what to do. But even when someone does, we don't take the advice we have been given. We are left with all our same ways of thinking and are back to where we started.

If there were such a thing as guaranteed solutions, like how some people make promises, we would not have a million different diet products. We wouldn't have a million self-help books and workshops. If there were a guaranteed solution, one formula would work so that we could all be OK in our lives and happy, achieving what our hearts desired.

Yet there is no single one-size-fits-all solution. You are on a journey that is unique to you. Along the way, you will have to figure things out on your own. No one can do it for you because your story belongs to you. But what this book can offer you is an understanding of yourself.

This book teaches you life is a process. It is part of your path along with every book you've read or will read, each workshop, meditation technique, inspiring podcast, and every time you forgive someone. Nothing is in vain. These are all small impressions that all make their mark until, collectively, they enable you to see things exactly for what they are and reach your moment as I did.

Anything can be confusing if we don't understand the processes we are going through, especially as we navigate our ships, sometimes with no instructions. This book provides you with the understanding that you can choose to be happy, and if you practice the key elements in it and implement them, you can make changes to make it happen.

About This Book

My purpose for writing *Understanding Your Life Purpose Triangle* is to help you have more clarity as you handle your life experiences so you can improve your life. The first few chapters provide insight into how we choose to be happy, the key elements of change by understanding the Life Purpose Triangle, and how this shows up for us in our lives through the processes we experience. Part III of the book describes how to apply the Life Purpose Triangle as it relates to many areas of life. And finally, in Part IV, the book discusses the connection between Life Purpose and your Authentic Self.

Before you read the book, I suggest you visit the book's Glossary to become familiar with the terms used throughout. You can always refer back to these terms. Reading the book and then rereading the chapters that resonate with you may be helpful. You may start to Self-Reflect and use some of the practises of the Triangle in your lives as you read. Or you may wish to read the book through first, then start to use your practises while referring back to the book as needed. I hope *Understanding Your Life Purpose Triangle* helps you realise you have the power within you to make necessary changes and to live a life with purpose.

PART I

HAPPINESS IS A CHOICE

Chapter 1
How Do You Choose to Live Your Life?

Happiness

Happiness. Everyone wants to be happy, but what does it actually mean? We all have our individual views on what it means to us. Some describe happiness as going on holiday, spending time with family and friends, going to the cinema, and playing sports—in other words, doing what we enjoy makes us happy.

Others may define happiness as having things: 'If I had my dream house, it would make me happy. If I found my perfect partner, I would be happy. If I had a lot of money, then I'd be happy.' Happiness has also been described as finding inner peace. But what is inner peace? Who defines inner peace?

Take a minute and think about where you are in your life right now. Let's start with your career, whatever that is to you—a permanent or part-time job, being a student or homemaker—anything associated with a career. Are you a hundred per cent satisfied? Is it everything you imagined it to be? Are you proud of the work you do on a daily basis? Does it make you happy?

Next, think about your relationships, from acquaintances to intimate ones. Are you experiencing loving, caring and trusting interactions? How about your body and your general health? Are you happy with your overall health and how you care for it?

Lastly, think about how you talk about your life to yourself and in conversations with others. Do you describe your life by saying it could be better, that life is hard and unfair? Do you feel you never get lucky chances, but everyone around you does? Or do you seem to attract many opportunities and experience life to be easy and purposeful?

Your Life is What You Make of It

What if I were to tell you that everything you are experiencing in your life right now, good or bad, is because of you? Every decision you have made in your life, no matter how insignificant it may seem, has led you to this point. You have created your relationships, the job you do every day, the current state of your health and every situation in your life, every single last one. You may disagree with me and say some things are not your fault; there were many terrible things that others have done to you.

Unfortunately, whether we are aware of it or not, consciously or subconsciously, we have made choices along the way that led us to the positions we are in. As for our initial experiences in life, such as who our families are, where we grew up or what circumstances we were born into, we didn't decide these. But anything after we started to make independent, conscious decisions for ourselves has determined our lives right now.

Your life has been moulded from all the decisions YOU have made. This is a pretty hard pill to swallow, especially if you are someone who has been trying to convince yourself that you do not have any choices in your life.

Yes, factors out of our control, like our early conditioning, society, culture, experiences, and other influences, have contributed to our current way of life. These may have influenced us greatly, and because of them, life sometimes may be difficult to comprehend. Some of our past circumstances may have been very challenging. If we were constantly exposed to negative and unfavourable circumstances, it might take the best of what is within us to be positive and not blame others for what happened.

I know life can be hard, painful, confusing, and frustrating. No one is taking those situations away, downplaying them or disregarding the pain anyone went through.

But no situation is meant to stay the same, not ever. If that were the case, humans would not evolve, and the world would not be where it is today. People would still be riding horses and in carriages or using lanterns for light.

We are not meant to stay in the same situations because we are always evolving. We are meant to learn, change and grow. If we are not doing this, we get stuck, remain in destructive repetitive patterns, and never move from this path.

Only you can choose to change the circumstances you are in.

Our World is Inside Out

Many of us have a belief that our world works from the outside in, yet our world is lived from the inside out. For example, we sometimes speak about the world and the people in it as if they're out there somewhere. We say things like, 'What is this world coming to?' We focus outside ourselves to explain why we are the way we are. Our view of life is that it is others out there in the world who are creating it, but the world is not out there. It comes from each of us. We all have created it. Though there is mistrust, unkindness, judgement, lack of love and negativity amongst us, there is also kindness, love, trust and compassion in this world.

If you are happy within, you project it out into the world. If you are sad within, you project that out. If it's your view to believe the world is never on your side, it won't be. If, because of your disadvantages in life, you think you never get opportunities, then you won't. Negative or positive outcomes occur due to your perspective. Your life depends on the lenses though which you see the world. You create your life from within.

Even so, we are led to believe that achievement and making changes in our lives either is blocked by the past or depends on some unknown future event. I constantly hear phrases from people like: 'If only I was raised differently. If I had this or that, then I could do what I have always wanted to do. I am waiting until next year when I will have things in order so I can do it.' You might be playing the fruit machines to win millions so you can finally change your life! We are waiting for some external thing to magically appear in our lives and wave a magic wand so all the things we view as obstacles disappear.

Once we take responsibility for our world, we can achieve whatever it is we want out of life. Nothing is unachievable—not ever. We are great and constantly achieving, but we will never truly see how much we do achieve simply because we are constantly evolving. Every time we achieve something, we go on to evolve and achieve something else.

We Get What We Wish For

Everything that you have wished for, you got. You just don't realise it when you get what you wish for. At one stage in your life, you wanted to learn how to walk—you did. Then you wanted to know how to ride a bike—you achieved it. Soon you wished for your first kiss, and you got it. When you earned your first pay cheque, you were super proud. And later, when you wanted a career, you achieved it. Everything in your world right now is what you consciously or unconsciously wished for.

You are attaining your goals and dreams every step of the way but may not acknowledge when they happen because they just don't feel big enough or grand enough or how your mind pictured them to be. There is no fancy firework display that is going to happen magically in your life to make you feel whole. You are the person you are and where you are because of all your good and bad experiences and all the learning and pain you had to go through. You *will* be reaching milestones in your journey. Recognise and celebrate each of your victories along the way. In so doing, you will stay grounded and appreciative.

So, celebrate you! Celebrate everything that has brought you to this point in your life right now, good and bad.

Two Ways to Live

People normally live their lives in two ways. The first is that they use what they have been through as an excuse or to explain a hindrance as to why they do the things they do. This generally leads to blaming others or adopting victim status. The second way is when someone takes their experiences and uses them, learns from them, understands them, but also takes responsibility for their part in situations. They do not blame anyone, not even themselves, so they move forward with a greater evolved mental maturity.

Human beings, at times, all love to have a good moan. They want others to feel sorry for them and sympathise with their story. It is natural to seek some attention and sympathy when we feel upset. This is very much normal, conditioned behaviour. But suppose you constantly blame others when things go wrong, make excuses when you find yourself in certain situations, and constantly look for some sympathy? Then you remain in a negative head space, your energy field is blocked and dark, and all you see is what you lack.

Choice

But why are their people who manage to become very successful in all aspects of their lives? Why are they able to change and not allow their conditioning and difficult experiences to affect them? How are they able to keep on growing their evolved mental maturity?

No one on this earth was born with superpowers like Superman. Everyone was born as an individual. Yes, we all have different gifts or things we may have become good at doing, either naturally or through dedicated work. But even someone born with talent will need commitment, consistency and effort to become even better at what they do. For example, someone may have been born with the natural, athletic ability to run very fast. But to become a sprinter and compete at the highest level takes tremendous training, patience and commitment. The person just doesn't wake up and become a sprinter through natural talent alone. In other words, no one was born with a superpower to be more successful than someone else. The difference between them and everyone else comes down to understanding CHOICE and how choice is used. With every experience in life, people have the freedom to choose.

Choice is a word and action that carries tremendous power—a power that each and every one of us has. It is our real superpower. We just can't comprehend the magnitude of such power because either we are conditioned to be unaware of it, or it simply sounds too easy. When we understand this power wholeheartedly, we start to live our best lives.

When you don't understand this power, you are choosing to believe that your ordeals in life weren't fair and that your influences and environment are very much to blame for your experiences. This is where you become stuck because you never learn that you *can* create opportunities for yourself. You are not living your best lives because few of you choose to accept your part in situations, and most of you think that life is what was done to you.

Once you understand choice and that you are always free to choose how you approach life, you will take the second path. When you go through hardships, you will choose to accept what happened, knowing it wasn't personal, even when you didn't deserve it, and that it wasn't a punishment and you are not bad because of it. You will choose to stop allowing and accepting bad experiences to govern who you are as a person. You will know what you decide at any moment will affect you later in life because you will understand that every conscious decision you are making about your life today will help you evolve to your next stage of growth.

More often than not, those who are very successful in all aspects of their lives have been through a great ordeal of some sort, yet no one would ever guess they had. They do not wear it as a badge of honour or use it as an excuse. They don't keep repeating their sorrowful story. Instead, they choose to see the good that came out of the turmoil and use it to help themselves and others. Of course, their experiences were not easy and, in fact, may have been the most difficult times in their lives. Did they endure feelings of fear, anxiety, doubt, worthlessness, hurt and sadness? Of course, they did. Even successful, strong people have conditioned thoughts and feelings, but the main difference is that they choose not to allow those feelings and thoughts to stop them from letting go and moving forward.

Successful people choose to see that they have the ability to move forward, not blame others, and try again, even if they fail. They choose to take responsibility when anything goes wrong in their lives and not to hate others or blame them for what they went through. They choose to see that if things go wrong, it is not a reflection of who they are but a learning experience and that they are not a failure, even if they may feel like it.

As the above illustrates, happiness comes from taking responsibility for our choices, including all the good or bad we have created. Living life from the inside out is the key. So is seeing that life is never as hard as we might think.

Chapter 2
Life is Not as Hard As It Seems

'Life is not as hard as it seems' is a statement that very few of us actually believe. Instead, as discussed in the previous chapter, people often describe life as hard and challenging. At various stages in my life, I, too, believed that's how life is. I thought that life had been very unfair to me. Not only did I believe that I'd never signed up for the experiences that had occurred in my life, but I also felt that I didn't deserve them.

When my life was not going according to what I wanted for it or to the plan I had envisioned for myself, I felt hurt and angry. I became an angry person. I was always projecting anger—in how I handled things, what I said, and in how I expressed what I felt. It was a long time before I learned to be the Observer of my life, take responsibility, accept what happened, and choose not to do things in the old way.

Tunnel Vision

Human beings make things far more complicated than they need to be. We form a view of how unfair life is to us, then find life to be that way, hard and challenging. We remain so focused on how we think things are meant to be that when they don't appear to be the way we want, we are not happy about it.

When we go through difficult times, we experience tunnel vision. We are like horses wearing blinkers in a race. We can't see what is around us, but only what is in front of us.

An analogy of this is finding yourself lost in a desert without access to water. You are all alone there with no one to help guide you in the right direction. It has been three days, and you still can't find any water. You have walked miles in the hope of finding some. It is only natural that you start to become despondent, angry, and annoyed as you become increasingly weak and dehydrated. You hate what's happening and wish this was not your reality! You feel as if you can't go on.

You see a hill in the distance, but this is about the fourth hill you have come across, got excited about, and climbed in the hope of finding some food and water. Each time before, though, once closer, what you saw was just more desert. You are tired and don't have the energy to get excited about another possibility, put in more effort, or get your hopes up again, only to discover there is no food or water.

Faced with making another decision, do you contemplate finding a spot in the sand to lay down on and accept you will never discover water, or do you keep going? Yet, something inside you—a feeling, a voice, a knowing—is telling you not to stop so you force yourself to go on. You climb, reach the top, and right before your eyes is the biggest stream with thousands of fruit trees around it.

When we are focused only on the negative view that hardships can create, it leaves very little room to see anything else. And over time, the more we believe we were unfairly mistreated, the more distorted our view of the hardships becomes.

For example, we may have created stories about our upbringing. We may have produced tunnel vision around our perceptions of them so that they became beliefs. This is why siblings raised in the same household by the same parents can all have different narratives about their upbringings.

Stacey grew up in a household with her two sisters. Her sisters were closer in age, but she was the eldest. She believed she got mistreated, and her two sisters didn't because she was older. She felt she was made to live out her mother's dreams and was forced to do things she didn't want to and expected to take on more responsibility than anyone else. Stacey felt it was unfair to her.

Her parents had given her many opportunities in life, like buying a business for her and her partner, supporting her financially, and continuing to support the emotional decisions she would make, even the ones they were against. Despite this, her entire life, Stacey kept replaying the narrative that she had been mistreated to herself. She even continued this narrative when telling her children stories about how unfair her life had been and how she hadn't had any choices and, in this way, she just created further mistruths.

Because Stacey didn't take responsibility or learn what was needed from her experiences, she remained in tunnel vision, and because of this, her tunnel vision view on any hardship kept her prisoner to her story. Her sisters did not view their childhood in the same way. They viewed it positively, recognizing the opportunities presented during it. And, even if there were things that could have been handled better, they did not carry resentments about it. Stacey has remained in tunnel vision and continues to believe she is justified in her story.

If you are unable to look back on experiences and see some good in the hardships, then you will remain in your tunnel vision.

When we experience 'tough situations', it is easy to become depressed and thus become stuck because we can't see the stream and trees beyond the hill. Because of this, we often perceive life to be hard. If you knew that the hill was hiding the water and trees, you would not view being lost in a desert without water as hard. You'd know, in that situation, your lesson is to keep climbing the hills even after failed attempts.

Those who have experienced some sort of hardship in their lives, and have come out the other side, have all said that it would not be something they would like to experience again but are glad it happened because it made them who they are. If most of us held this view, we wouldn't constantly complain about how unfair life is or worry endlessly. We should all believe and understand that, no matter the reason or lesson for our next challenging experience, we will eventually be able to again find that hill that provides us with everything we need.

We have so many options, resources, endless choices and possibilities in life, but we can remain stuck and keep allowing ourselves to keep the blinkers on. We blindly remain in our tunnel vision until we learn what we need to know. Once we have learnt the lesson of an experience, we are then able to look back at the situation without any blinkers on and move on and view our next experiences with a new lens.

What We Get

Sometimes, what we think we want is not necessarily what we need. When the universe gives you something not in your envisioned plan, there is a reason for it. You just may not be able to understand what it is yet because of where you are in your ability to take responsibility and observe the effects of your actions. Being more open-minded and trusting in how life and situations will work out is crucial to existence.

Life is as hard or as easy as you make it. Your state of mind will determine this. The question is, how are you going to view life? Will you only see miles of desert around you with impossible hills to climb? Or will you view life with miles of desert around you with hills that could provide opportunity? Where are you going to put your focus? Because your focus could keep you in a desert, living a life that verges on barely living. What are you going to choose?

Chapter 3
Self-Worth and Belief

I once had a conversation with a lovely girl who was my work colleague at the time. We were speaking casually about what we wanted out of life—our goals, wants, and desires. During the conversation, I listed all the things I wanted to achieve—it was a pretty long list. After listening to what I wanted, she looked at me and told me that she wasn't greedy and would be happy with only one thing. I knew she wanted more. With further questioning, I asked what her reasoning was for only wanting one thing. She said she had a greater chance of getting one thing than ten. This conversation saddened me because I know there are so many who, like her, limit themselves in so many ways because of their lack of self-worth and belief. People form a belief that they are asking for too much if they want more.

Belief

Your sense of self-worth and what you believe can be so powerful that they can take you to great heights, but they can also have a negative impact on you. Belief is your core. It will outline your view of the world and is one of the key fundamentals that determine your mindset. Belief can also limit the way you view things.

A common belief that many of us often fall prey to is thinking our lives are destined to only be a certain way. This is especially reinforced when we experience certain challenging circumstances. We may find ourselves experiencing the same situations over and over again and feel like we never seem to get what we want. Or we may be unable to put ourselves forward even when we believe we deserve what we want. When things get tough, our limited belief and low self-worth often deters our progress.

But belief is needed for you to carry on walking through the desert and climbing your hills after many failed attempts. We live in a world with thousands of billionaires and millions of millionaires, all co-existing with us. Yet here we are, some of us only asking for one thing in the hope of it coming true.

Having materialistic things in life, like money and assets, is a side effect of our goals and achievements, which are a reflection of our beliefs. If you want to obtain the side effects like wealth that come with achievements, you will need to work on your belief.

Do you think those who have succeeded in becoming billionaires only ever asked for one thing? No, of course, they didn't. They had many hopes and desires. If you believe that you will only ever be good enough for certain things in life, then that will happen, and if you believe, just like my work colleague did, that you stand more of a chance of getting one thing rather than many, then it will be one thing you will get.

Mindset is Your Greatest Weapon

Your belief and self-worth can never be taken from you. As discussed, the only person stopping you from achieving what you want is you. Maintaining a positive mindset is just as important as holding fast to positive belief and self-worth. Your mindset is among your greatest weapons, so carry on believing that you are worthy in every way, carry on believing you will always find the stream and the fruit trees no matter what and watch how things unfold in miraculous ways.

Sometimes we find ourselves in situations where we know what we want and believe what we want is true to us, yet our social environment tells us that it's wrong. This can cause us to feel stuck, confused and lost because our wishes and desires are not in line with what we have been taught. When we move forward in pursuing what we want, we may be faced with the struggle of going against everything we have come to know and backlash from the people we love and want approval from. These conflicts can influence our self-worth and belief even when we work hard to stay in a positive mindset.

No one on this earth has all the answers. Life is full of unanswered questions and so many unknowns. Sadly, all this uncertainty only leads some to judge others because they truly believe what they think is correct. While this can feel very limiting to the many who feel differently than others or how they were brought up, it is vital to remain true to yourself and find others of your belief.

Since these are sensitive matters, I don't want to write in-depth about religion, culture, ethnicity, sexuality and gender because then I might seem to be passing judgement on those who have strong beliefs in what they consider to be correct. But our self-worth can be impacted by these influences.

We can only make changes and take responsibility for our part in situations. If others want to pass cruelty and judgement onto us, this is because of their own conditioning, learnt experiences, and where their evolved mental maturity is. We can only offer them love and compassion in return.

If you are dealing with confusing feelings, please reach out and seek help. No one should struggle with confusing thoughts alone because you are not alone. Remember, you are an individual, so whatever you feel within is for you, and what you feel is justified in every way.

How do we push through the boundaries of upbringing and society to achieve more? How do we nurture and grow our self-worth? Some of us genuinely believe we have strong self-worth and belief, while others might feel that they don't have any.

Fully aligning with our self-worth is accepting nothing less than what you feel you need.

Mixed Signals

When our belief is conflicted, or we don't believe we deserve what we want, we send out mixed signals to the universe. A good example of this concerns one of the most common predicaments we find ourselves in—finding our dream life partner.

Perhaps you have expressed you want to have a meaningful, loving and respectful relationship. You've listed the top five qualities you are looking for in someone to match your needs. Then you meet someone with three out of the five qualities on your list. You think, 'Good enough', and start dating them. Or you tell people, 'Well, they are OK. They are the closest to what I have been looking for in a long while, and I could change what's missing about them later on.'

You say you want certain things, yet you still accept and allow what you don't want in your life. Somewhere along the way—after hundreds of failed dates, years of rejection, all the tiresome effort of searching—you gave up believing that the person you are looking for and deserve is still out there for you. This sends mixed signals. You can't truly be aligning with your self-worth if you still accept some of the things you don't want.

Another example of how you contradict your wants and belief is if you may be at a point in your life where you have found yourself in a job or occupation that you have outgrown yet stay in it. Maybe you have spent a good few years in that job or pursuing that occupation and know very well that it isn't supporting your growth anymore. Instead of leaving, you think, 'At least I have a job. It pays the bills. I suppose I just need to be grateful. There are people out there who are worse off than I am.' Being grateful for your current job is very important because there was a time when you really wanted that job. But do not accept the situation if it is not making you happy. This doesn't mean to go hand in your notice tomorrow, but it does mean focusing on what you do want and making a plan to achieve it.

Never give up on anything that you want, and never settle for something. As the examples above show, settling means you don't truly believe you are worthy of more. Settling is a form of giving up. Not only does it send mixed signals to the universe, it is outright directing the universe that it doesn't have to carry on sending you things because you have accepted your situation.

Make the Necessary Changes

The most fundamental lesson we can learn to help build our self-worth and belief is to have the honesty, fight and courage to let go of situations we know we don't want. If a friend takes you for granted, don't just think, 'I will make do with what I have as I don't have any friends.'

This is not how life works. You have to show the universe you mean business! You know your self-worth and what you deserve. Let the universe know you won't stop until your needs are met because you deserve everything your heart desires. If you continue to accept things in part, you are preventing yourself from moving in the direction you need to go. Continuing to live your life this way is like choosing the route of a journey on Google maps that takes 1 hour and 40 minutes rather than the route that can get you there in 50 minutes. It may even be that if you take the long way around, you'll have to repeat the trip until you learn how to get there the fastest way.

Part of understanding and knowing your self-worth is putting in the effort to make the changes necessary to give yourself exactly what it is you desire. And that is letting go of situations even when they feel familiar and comfortable. What if you feel as though you are incapable of putting in the effort to make the necessary changes? Realize that you can do it because you do it for others, even if you may not be doing it for yourself.

Every one of us has had, at some point, people in our lives who we love and would do anything for, like our children, close family members, a friend, or a partner. We love them dearly and know what their dreams and desires are. There isn't a single doubt in our minds that would stop us from doing anything for them. We have understood their worth, believed in and loved them so much that we supported them in any way necessary to help make their goals a reality. Now give that same level of love and adoration that you muster for those you love to yourself. Put that same amount of effort and belief into your own self-worth.

Reinforcing Belief

So, how do you know what true self-belief feels like? Real belief in yourself needs to have the same quality of feeling and determination as in the following analogy. Imagine you are entering a dark room. The darkness is total, and you are unable to see anything. You know the light switch is located at the opposite side of the room, so you enter and are prepared to walk to the other side in the dark, not knowing what may be there, but with the full knowing, belief, and trust that once you get there, you will be able to find the switch and turn it on to light the room. There was never a doubt in your mind that you would ever be left in the darkness.

Sometimes we will experience situations where we feel like we are in the dark. At these times, we have to believe there will always be a light switch. The most important part of our belief is also allowing and trusting that what we want will manifest in ways that will always work out for us, though part of that might be in ways totally different to what we had envisioned.

Don't get disheartened when things don't appear as you imagined. It's okay to feel upset, but don't allow it to influence or deter you or affect your self-worth and belief. There could be lessons for your emotional and mental evolution (see the next section on Evolved Mental Maturity) that need working on. It may be that you still need to fully embrace what you are asking for. Not receiving a certain goal should never affect your self-worth.

The Magnificence That Is You

Self-worth is knowing you are a magnificent being and deserve everything in abundance in every aspect of your life. Those who eventually go on and succeed in achieving their goals and desires did not stop until they did. Your self-worth and belief are partly responsible for determining your life. If they are crushed or low, or if you don't fully understand the importance and magnificence that is you, then you must address this as much as you can.
I offer encouragement to you if you are going through an inner battle that is causing you to have feelings of worthlessness, whether due to what others around you are telling you or your past experiences. Know that all the answers lie within. You are unique; there is a reason why you have been called to question how you feel about yourself and your life. Don't live your life based on fear (discussed more in Chapter 14), but live it with courage. Do what makes you happy; if you live your life for everyone else and not yourself, you will never truly be happy.

True self-worth is wholeheartedly knowing that you can achieve and receive whatever you desire. Self-worth is to respect and love yourself enough to let go of the things that are not working for or completing your life, even if they feel comfortable. Always believe in yourself, and never give up on yourself.

Chapter 4
Your Evolved Mental Maturity

We have been discussing ways to look at life and create what we want. These include realising that choice is paramount, not looking at life as though it is a hardship, and the critical importance of positive belief and self-worth. All of these contribute to your Evolved Mental Maturity.

We belong to the human race, so we are part of a family and all connected in one way or another. But we are still all *individuals*—we are not part of a batch of identical items. We must each understand that we are extremely rare.

No one else is like you; you are unique to you and everyone else around you. This means you have your own perceptions and unique perspective. There are also specific lessons you are meant to learn and experience while alive. You can't know with certainty why your lessons are the ones they are—it is just one of the beautiful mysteries of life.

What is It?

Here is a simple analogy to understand what Evolved Mental Maturity is. Before you were born, without you knowing it, you were entered to run twenty 10k races in your life. You will have specific challenges in your races, and how you tackle them will affect all your future races. In your very first race, you had no idea you were going to run a race and had little experience and knowledge about running. So you ran your first race very slowly, stopping and starting continuously. It took you 2 hours to finish the race. Such was the level of your ability.

After running the first race, you knew you had another race to run, but from your experience in the first race, you realised that you were unfit and needed to put in a little more effort by doing some training. You decide that going for a run once a week might help you get fitter and possibly do better in your next race, so you choose to have the discipline to do so.

In your second race, you still start and stop, but with the little extra effort you put in because of your first experience, you do slightly better, and manage to run your race in 1 hour and 50 minutes. You are pleased with yourself and can feel the changes in your body.

By the third race, you start speaking to another runner who shares some knowledge with you, suggests putting in even more extra effort during the week, and invites you to join them in training three times a week. So, you decide to do that. You finish your third race in 1 hour 30 minutes. Now you feel a bit more confident, have more determination, and believe that you might be able to do the next race in 1 hour and 15 minutes. So, you spend a bit more time researching to help yourself improve, continue to put more effort in, and get better each time.

The person that you were in race one is different from the person who ran race three. You have more experience, understanding, confidence and belief. The person who ran race one would be unable to run race four or five if they did not take part in races two and three. With each race came experience and knowledge but also the decision to make the effort to run a better race—you evolved in each race.

Similarly, in life, we are all running our own individual races, and what they are and where we are is unique to us. This means we are all at different levels in our Evolved Mental Maturity in life, and how we contribute to any situation is due to our individual experiences. Only each of us can run our own races. No one else can run our races for us.

If you find yourself dissatisfied with any of the experiences you have had or are experiencing, then it is you who can also make the needed changes to do better in your next race.

Everyone Evolves at Their Own Pace

So in life, each and every one of us is experiencing a different Evolved Mental Maturity. We are all running our races and deciding how to run our next races.

If people disappoint you or you feel dissatisfied in a relationship, wanting or needing more from another person, remember they have their own Evolved Mental Maturity, and it may not align with yours. It isn't their fault. Just remember, the growth of their Evolved Mental Maturity will be at their own pace in their own race, so whatever they do is all they know right now. They could not run race eight if they were only equipped with the knowledge of what they needed to put in and do in race two. Even if you still feel what happens between you should be different, what they do is all they can do at this time.

Similarly, suppose you find yourself at a more Evolved Mental Maturity level, one where, looking back, you feel that if you had been in the other person's shoes, you would have done better in the relationship than they did. Yet, just imagine the feelings that they were left with, knowing that they had failed you.

Realize, too, that there are those who may have fallen during their first race over some stones in their path, which made them fearful or contributed to an injury. If you went to watch a long-distance race and someone tripped, fell and was in pain, would you ignore them, be angry and shout at them? No, you wouldn't. You would go over and help them up. So try to remember we are all running individual races at the evolvement level we have been able to learn and acquire up to this point—no more.

Offering understanding and compassion instead of having feelings of frustration, annoyance, anger, and blame proves that you have evolved. Be grateful that you have the ability and the tools to make the needed efforts for that relationship race. With the gifts that you have, offer love, forgiveness, and support to those still struggling with their races instead of judgement, anger and hate.

This concludes Part I. We've covered how happiness is a choice and how where we are in our lives is due to our past choices. We've discussed belief and self-worth as well as Evolved Mental Maturity. Armed with these ideas and how they contribute or not to our happiness, we move on to the tools that will help you bring about the change you want to see in your world.

PART II

THE KEYS TO CHANGE

Chapter 5
We Need to Self-Reflect

I remember reading: 'Don't judge me on my past as I am not that person anymore.' We often use phrases like, 'I have changed. I am a different person than I used to be.' But as we run our races and develop our Evolved Mental Maturity, do we truly change and become someone else, or are we like computer programs that need regular updates? Computer programs are updated because issues, like security flaws, have been discovered or improvements created. Improving current features or creating new ones is very similar to how we learn and evolve.

As individuals evolve, so does humanity. It is evident that, through the generations, there have been many practices that formerly existed, but people realised that there are better ways of doing things and so made changes for the better. Take, for example, corporal punishment in schools, when you were physically struck as punishment if you misbehaved. Not all teachers got it right. Some could take hitting children to the extreme based on their emotions, which often had nothing to do with the children's behaviour. Over time, people evolved in understanding and recognising that some children had learning difficulties and were not misbehaving. The view became that corporal punishment was cruel, and some children needed specialist care and attention. This was one part of a social system that was corrected.

Correct Our Conditioning

In our own lives, we come from familial, cultural, and belief systems given to us in childhood. We also all have had experiences in our early lives that have impacted how we behave as adults. This becomes our conditioning. But it is not set in stone, just as in the example above about how society grows and changes; we, too, can grow and change.

Sometimes, our most painful experiences occurred because the behaviours we displayed in these situations came from our conditioning. For example, as a child, your very first experience of understanding a romantic relationship came from watching your parents. Through observation, you subconsciously were learning about personal relationships. When you encounter your first personal relationship, the behaviours you display will stem from the relationships you had around you growing up.

Suppose when you were a child, your father was quite controlling, domineering, spoke down to your mother, and didn't spend much time at home. When you enter your first long-term relationship, subtly, unconsciously, you behave in a similar way. When things don't work out, and your partner decides to leave, it has ended for a reason. And part of that reason is for you to discover that it is your behaviour that needs changing. You need to learn how to be in a positive, loving, balanced relationship, not like the one you were taught, not like how you were conditioned. But to be able to understand and learn this, you will need to do a lot of Self-Reflecting.

For example, you may have grown up in a household where the behaviours, actions, and habits of the adults around you were not in line with what you believed to be true. Some of their behaviours left you feeling hurt or may have affected your self-worth. As you grew up, you started to realise there were better ways of doing things. You decided that, as soon as you were responsible for your own actions and had an influence on others, you would do things differently and create positive behaviours. You examined your conditioning and changed your behaviours based on your experience. In each generation, there are those trying to change the conditioning they received from the generation before.

It is magical that many, if they were mistreated in certain ways as children, absolutely do want to change things for the better for their children. They consistently raise their children differently from how they were raised. But why only limit changing your conditioning to just how you approach your children or family? How about extending this to everyone, including strangers and those who hurt us?

Evolving means we carry this process on in the experiences we create in our lives—we learn from them, make the necessary changes about ourselves, and then apply those changes.

Look in the Mirror

If you were to really think about what you'd like to be different about yourself, you would come to realise that the changes you want to make are, in fact, damaging behaviours. Behaviours you had no idea you were doing or expressing as part of who you are.

We all have a part to play on this earth, and we can choose to be willing to learn and make the changes necessary to be the loving beings we are. Or we can stay in the same repeated patterns. But to stop the cycles of conditioning, we have to understand one of the fundamental processes of change on this earth—Self-Reflection.

Because we don't always know how our behaviours originated and can't always pinpoint what lessons we are meant to learn, it is of the utmost importance to Self-Reflect.

Self-Reflection is key to changing our conditioned ways and learning our lessons.

Self-Reflection is taking responsibility for the part we play in situations. It is looking in the mirror without blame, the blame of others and ourselves. Self-Reflection helps us understand our conditioning. And our conditioning is part of our Influencer Self which will be explained in the next chapter.

To truly and deeply Self-Reflect, we must make it a priority to take some time out of every day to think through our experiences and let go of all the things that do not serve us. Only then can we understand the real reasons why we behave the way we do. We can change our behaviour, but it does take consistent effort because Self-Reflecting can leave us feeling vulnerable. **Sometimes with vulnerability comes a return to conditioned behaviour.**

What We Can Change

There is so much in life we cannot change. We think we need to teach those who mistreat us. We think we need to stand up for ourselves and prove our points to everyone. We even believe we need to act and be a certain way to be accepted or make others like us. None of this matters, nor will it change anything. The only thing that you need to concentrate on is what changes *you* can make within yourself.

When you change how you think and behave instead of focusing on what others out there are doing or have done, your life will flow in a positive way. This is what results from Self-Reflection. You concentrate on yourself and your own life. It also allows you to work alongside your Observer Self.

Chapter 6
Becoming the Observer

Self-Reflection enables you to work with your Observer Self. Once you practise reflecting on situations that have occurred in your life, you will become more and more adept at engaging in such reflection in the moment. This is stepping into your Observer Self. If you want to make changes in your life, the process must include becoming the Observer of your life. Then you can finally live a life that is purposeful and meaningful to you.

Being the Observer Self means to view yourself as if from the outside and watch who you are in a situation as it is happening. And it is deciding how you will act or respond to the experience only from this vantage point. When you step outside of your thoughts and known conditioning, you can look at what is happening objectively.

We all know that when it comes to anyone else's problems, we are the best at giving advice—yet we seldom take our own inner advice when we ought to. Your friends' problems seem pretty black-and-white because it isn't your emotions involved, nor is it your conditioning. You see their problem or issues clearly for what they are—you are the Observer. This is what you need to learn to do with your own inner and outer worlds, being the Observer of your thoughts and actions as if you are on the outside 'looking in'.

It is also possible to engage the Observer Self even before you participate in a situation. Such situations could be anything from leaving your house in the morning, engaging in certain conversations, disciplining your children, and deciding what to eat or how much exercise to do. Being the Observer is almost like having an out-of-body experience. It allows you to observe your self then decide how you will proceed.

Understand Your Influencer

Some of what the Observer Self brings to us is the ability to identify our Influencer. Sometimes it is almost a shock to discover we all have an Influencer since most of us go through life having no clue about it.

Our Influencer Self holds all our habits, patterns and conditioning from when they were initially created, but we have no recollection of how that all happened. It is where all our self-identifying thoughts and labels originated and where we harbour guilt, shame, self-justification, and arrogance. The Influencer loves to manipulate, blame, get angry and self-destruct.

This is the part of us that learnt to fear and use substitutions such as food, gambling, or drink to check out of our lives. Our Influencer wants to put up walls to protect us. Because our Influencer is where our insecurities live, it created our comfort zone, which so limits us and all our possibilities. It is also what people describe as our egos.

The Influencer has learnt many things that are not in our best interest. This includes how it has developed associations with things. For example, it believes reasons other than the truth about why certain things happened in our lives. Because of the Influencer, we might live according to these associations for a long time. Though seemingly all very innocent in its workings, it influences us by providing false narratives because all it learnt was based on misunderstandings. This is the part of the brain where we generally go back and forth in inner discussions about whether we should do something or not. In this manner, the Influencer can impact all your decision-making processes.

Your Influencer believes it is acting in ways that always serve you, but it doesn't. It genuinely believes it is not causing you any harm. Sometimes it feels like it needs to protect you and keep you safe. Other times it thinks it is being kind to you, showing you and others genuine love. It can be reactive at times as well as unreactive and accepting.

The Influencer Self is discussed throughout this book. The next section details the many aspects of your life that contributed to creating it. These include your childhood and environments like school and social media. Your Influencer affects how you choose to live your life in almost all ways—your fears, habits, wants, and desires; how you perceive love and time; the need for control and uncertainty; your quick-fix mentality; and how things show up for you.

If you are to grow, learn and evolve, one of your most important tasks in life is to understand your Influencer, all the things it does that don't serve you, and allow it to be released.

Your Observer Recognizes Your Influencer

Observation is how you recognise your Influencer, such as when it reacts to something you feel someone is doing to you, but in fact, no harm is meant. Your Observer Self understands your Influencer Self is just reacting to past experiences and that something in your new situation has triggered an old feeling.

Being the Observer, you can see when you are acting out of your vulnerabilities and know you are being manipulative because you want to get your own way. The Observer sees you are starting a fight because you feel scared and threatened, yet instead of telling the other person this, you are making it about something irrelevant. Being the Observer is that part of you that knows you are running away from something because it frightens you, but you give yourself some other excuse for it. In all these situations, the Observer knows that the Influencer is at work.

Here is an example many have experienced. One morning you arrive at work and walk into the staff room. You find your work colleagues engaged in conversation, walk over, say hello, and stand there listening to them. They are all gossiping about another work colleague (whom you don't have any ill will toward) and saying not-very-nice things about them. Standing there and listening at that moment is when you will need to be the Observer.

Having noticed what is being said, you now have to make a choice. You know it's not right to speak badly about others, so you observe, and before speaking, ask yourself, Do I join in the negativity? Do I walk away, or do I try to diffuse the situation? This is the observation process. At times like these, you will need to decide how you want to engage and participate in your life.

In addition to observing yourself in the moment, your Observer Self can connect to what your Influencer Self is doing after situations have occurred as well. Whenever you notice you feel guilt, remorse, or feel as though you have been bad, then know your Observer Self is at work because you are able to Self-Reflect. For example, sometimes you can react to situations out of annoyance, anger, sadness, frustration, and hurt—it is immediate without any thought process because it is projected from your subconscious. But after you have cooled off or calmed down, you feel bad for how you reacted or what you said since your Observer is now seeing it.

Your Responsive Self

So, when you choose to become more present in your life and learn to work with your Observer Self, the next step is to become acquainted with your Responsive Self. When your Observer Self makes you aware of situations, your Responsive Self has a choice in whether or how you are going to react or respond. How you choose to respond in situations will either move you back to your Influencer Self or help move you into your Authentic Self.

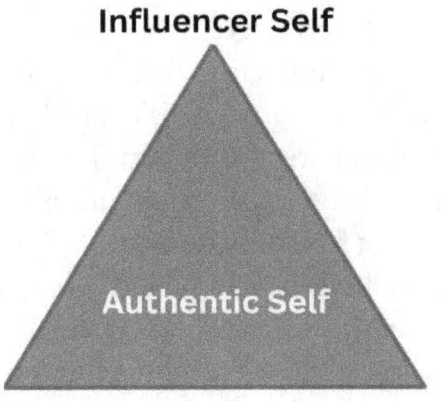

Your Life Purpose Triangle

We know we can say certain things to hurt people and get reactions. Equally, we do have the capacity to know what we are doing in situations. Of course, our Observer Selves will not be able to catch our Influencer Selves all the time, but this is OK because our Responsive Selves can still choose to apologise and ask for forgiveness for our actions, identify the behaviour, and change it in the future.

Regarding the previous example, how will your Responsive Self choose to react, if at all? Will it join in the negative office gossip, choose not to engage, or rather decide to be about empowering people?

Authentic Self

Once you are able to truly be your Observer Self, you will be able to identify the difference between your Authentic Self and Influencer Self. What is it to be authentic? The word *authentic* is defined as something that is genuine and original. In regards to people, it comes with an element of freedom that is pure and legitimate. Living from the Authentic Self means that everything you do feels right. The choices you make are unattached and not deceptive or innocently influenced by the conditions you were exposed to. You are forgiving to everyone in your life who may have caused you some upset, as you do not see what they may have done as an attack but a misguided choice.

Once you align with your Authentic Self, an overwhelming feeling of joy and purity fills your heart.

There is a sense of peace in what you say, feel, and do. Everything feels as though it is meant to be, has its place, and is happening exactly how it should. Everything feels aligned. You feel grounded and undisturbed by restlessness or any overwhelming feelings because you know everything will work out exactly as it is meant to.

You know you are being taken care of and that everything is great. When you speak, it is a truth that is governed by love. You are all about love, nothing else, and you can feel the powerful force of connection that is living on this earth, which has always been living here before tunnel vision arose in humans' minds.

To truly find your purpose is to align with your Authentic Self first.

The more you choose to respond in ways that align with your Authentic Self, the more natural it will become. Your brain will become familiar with this way of thinking and eventually store your new habit. Over time, choosing to do acts of positivity in all situations in your life eventually breaks you away from your negative habits. Your Influencer begins to understand that what it did before, like providing safety, is no longer required. It does take persistent effort, though; it doesn't happen overnight.

Being in your Observer and Responsive Selves, changing your habits, and moving away from old ways takes effort, so you have to work at it consistently. It is not something you choose to do on a Monday morning and revisit again in a week. Be kind and patient with yourself, as you won't get it right all the time. Your Influencer will try to go back to its learned behaviour because it's familiar. But as you evolve and work in aligning with your Authentic Self, your Authentic Self will become more familiar. Next, we will discuss another key element in working with your Life Purpose Triangle, which is practising gratitude.

Chapter 7
Remember to Always Be Thankful

Human beings are able to dream and create things that were once beyond the imagination. If we could go back in time and bring people who lived in the 1900s to visit the world today, they would be astonished and blown away by how the world is now. Mankind has certainly evolved since then, and milestones are continuously still being reached. Humans will continue to evolve in magnificent ways, and similarly, you continue to evolve in what you want out of life.

Wanting More

We always want more. Wanting more is a natural process in life—once you learn one thing, you go on to learn another. We also have the amazing ability to adapt to many situations. Part of our ability to learn and move forward contributes to bringing us closer to the next part of our evolvement. It's great that we can do this, but having this ability means we may get caught up with always wanting more for the wrong reasons, which can leave us feeling dissatisfied or unfulfilled.

People will go into a career, learn all that is required in the position, then after a few years, ask for a progression because of wanting to learn more—this is a natural process. But on the flip side, the need to want more also relates to our social context and materialism.

For instance, you bought a mobile phone two months ago, but the company you bought the phone from has just advertised a newer model, which will be coming out in the next few months. Absolutely nothing is wrong with your existing phone, but the latest version has features that you just can't do without. We do this with fashion trends too. We don't want unbranded trainers costing only five pounds; we want a well-known, branded trainer—this makes us feel like we are cooler, so we feel more accepted.

Everyone has been in a position of truly wanting something that cost more than they could afford. Months of saving may have been required before they were finally in a position to purchase it. It could have been anything from a really expensive watch to a handbag, trainers, holiday, or piece of jewellery.

Suppose this is you. Once you got to the point where you could buy the thing you wanted, gosh, you were ecstatic. You felt like a kid on Christmas morning and couldn't believe that you were finally going to get what you wanted. You bought it, feeling so happy. It was everything you had desired. Then a year later, the very item that you so desperately wanted, that you just couldn't go without, that took months and months of effort in saving, gets pushed to the back of a drawer, and you replace it with something else. Eventually, years later, it finds its way down to the charity shop.

Outgrowing Things

We lose interest in everyday situations in life, too—like taking a job for granted. You might find yourself at a stage in life where you are in a job that you have probably outgrown and are ready to move on. However, there may be certain circumstances that don't immediately allow you to move jobs yet. You start to get annoyed at any little thing. Every day you leave work and speak negatively, moaning about your co-workers and complaining about how much work there is, and your resentment towards your current job grows stronger each day. In fact, you may have even often said: 'I hate my job.'

You don't remember there was a time in your life when your current job was the very thing that you so eagerly wanted. You wished and prayed while waiting for that phone call or email notifying you if you got the job or not. When you got it, you were over the moon. You probably went out and celebrated.

Unfortunately, we do this with almost everything we outgrow. What we want today is not what we want tomorrow—we can be very complex at times. Do not allow yourself to turn what you have outgrown into negative energy. Instead, give thanks to your current situation, even while you are being clear that you are ready to move onto your next evolvement. Changing what you say from 'I hate my job' to 'Thank you for the job I have. I appreciate my job as it was once what I wanted; however, I am now ready for my next step' keeps your situation in the positive rather than the negative.

Practising Gratitude

Learning to practice gratitude for what is in our lives, even when we are ready to move on, helps us remain happy and content in the now. Showing gratitude and thanks allows us to recognise and remind ourselves of the effort and work it took for us to be where we are and have what we have. It stops us from feeling any resentment because it reminds us that the very situation we are currently resenting is what we once wished for.

When we are in a state of always giving thanks, we are reminded of the good around us, which keeps us in a state of happiness. This is very important because most of the time, we are almost always in a state of wanting more.

Living in the now will not keep you stuck or from accomplishing future goals and desires. You can still think about your plans. But if you do not show gratitude, you are not reminded of all you have, how far you have come and how much you have already achieved. If you do not show continuous gratitude, you will always be living in the future and experiencing feelings of anxiety and of never having enough. The important thing to remember when practising gratitude and giving thanks is that there is never any lack.

This Part II, The Keys to Change, presented the most important tools for developing awareness so that you can make changes in yourself and your life. Self-Reflection and Observation help you understand how your Influencer and Responsive Selves can undermine you. Meanwhile, consciously being grateful keeps you positive and assists you in moving forward.

As we have discussed, change does not happen overnight. It requires consistent effort and process to understand your Influencer and its conditioning. To assist you in this process, the next section, Part III, The Process, describes the many aspects of your life that you may choose to examine to better understand your Influencer. It explains how these areas have contributed to creating our Influencer Self.

Part III includes discussions about how our childhood and labels may have affected us and how our surroundings, like school, social media, and the consumer market, may have also impacted us. It also discusses how to approach our fears and uncertainty, wants and desires, relationships, perceptions of love and time, and the habits we need to release our comfort zones.

Part III

The Process

Chapter 8
From the Very Beginning

There is Only One You

Even with billions of people living on Earth, *you* have a very special place here. There is only one *you*, and there will only ever be one of *you*. There isn't anyone else in the world with the same fingerprint as you—not even identical twins have the same fingerprint. That is pretty incredible, don't you think? Close your eyes for a second and just think about it—there is no one else out there like you—*only you*. You are extremely important. You have an involvement in and influence on this earth, no matter how small or insignificant you think you are.

This also means, naturally, that we have tremendous power and strength. But unfortunately, nowadays, many of us think very little of ourselves and never think we aren't worthy of anything. Many factors may have contributed to why we might feel this way. Some of them are the influences around us when we were growing up.

To unravel our conditioning, we need to go back to where it all began. That's not to say that everyone was affected badly in childhood, but for many of us, looking closely at our childhood provides some answers.

We All Have a Story

We all have a story. Our story begins when we were young and includes our earliest memories, what we did then and experiences along the way up until now. Most of us have stories and can explain in great detail what we did in our lives, who we think we are and what we would still like to do. Some of the stories we have created can be extremely complex.

Sometimes we do certain things in life because of the stories we have created, and, at times, we can connect to our stories in ways that do not serve us. We can become too attached to our stories, as though we are the victims of them. However, if we know how to recognise and understand our stories, then we will be able to forgive, let go and learn that they don't need to affect us in any way. We can use our story to serve us instead.

How You Were Raised

Our existence in this world has been influenced by the home we were raised in. We were taught our parents' thoughts and beliefs and by their actions. This ultimately means that we all have some sort of conditioning that has contributed to who we are today.

Right from the beginning, from the very day they were born, a person entered this world with two parents. Some parents planned to have their children, and others didn't. Some children were raised by both parents, others by adoption, one parent, same-sex parents, or through foster care. Were you perhaps one of those children who was told or found out by chance that you were a 'mistake'? That you weren't meant to be here, that no one was ready for you?

Every child wants to feel wanted and loved. Yet, with so many different narratives even before they are born, it is only natural that people question their existence and importance. Children are very impressionable; they admire their parents so much when they are young. Ever hear a child say, 'I want to be just like mummy' or 'I want to be just like daddy'? They are constantly watching the world around them, learning and following the example of those who raised them. They want to be like their parents, so over time, they learn their traits.

You did this very same thing, too; you were once such a child. The adults around you were your teachers growing up, and you put your parents on pedestals from a very young age, believing they had all the answers and couldn't put a foot wrong. You wanted and craved their attention, acknowledgement, and love. But, if you didn't get these or what you now feel you needed at the time, then you can allow this to affect you.

Becoming an adult, especially when you are trying to figure everything out on your own without any manual, can be challenging at times. Without realising it, you can find yourself acting exactly like your parents did. Or, you could be aware that things at home were not for your best. This could be related to anything, for example, being called a nickname you hated, constantly being told you were useless, the tone used when they spoke to you, or the rules imposed on you. It might have left you feeling uncared about, and you still carry these feelings as an adult without knowing it.

Parents are only the vessels that are used for children to be born. We will learn certain things from them to help us become adults. However, parents unconsciously can try to live their goals and dreams through us. Most people who have not dealt with things from when they were young either repeat what happened through behaviour or self-talk or go to the opposite extreme, leading to overcompensation.

Jacky's Conditioning Around Food

Jacky is a lovely, warm lady who always got on well with others, and children loved her. As a child, Jacky's mother believed that children should not be allowed any sweets. Jacky was often left out at birthday parties, sleepovers, and any sort of gathering. Jacky always felt excluded, and this made her believe she was different— she was the strange girl who could not have any sweets. Children would laugh at her and call her names. This hurt her deeply.

When Jacky became a parent of her own, she promised herself that she would never do to her children what her mother had done to her. She allowed her children to have as many sweets as they wanted. There was no restriction. They could have sweets for breakfast or before bed if they so wished. But it was not only limited to sweets. Jacky allowed her children and herself to overindulge in food.

Jacky and her children became unhealthily overweight. Her hurtful experience made her go totally the opposite way, but not in a healthy, positive way to make a change for the better. Unfortunately for Jacky, she had not worked through the emotions she had felt as a child, and instead of making the situation better, she had made it worse. She had been conditioned one way, yet she was also conditioning her children in another way.

Sometimes the way we approach the past to change things is not always for the better. In Jacky's case, she tried to reflect and recognise what didn't work for her, but because she was acting out of hurt and pain and had not worked through her pain correctly, it negated what she was trying to do. Her parents taught her in a way that she didn't particularly like (due to their own conditioning), and Jackie just created further behavioural patterns in her children. It is important to understand, accept, and release the situations we view as painful.

Continuing to Remain Angry

Even though we have been influenced, everyone is born with a personality all their own, making them unique. Each person has fundamental inner core values that are part of who they are, different from anyone else's. Some people will speak positively of their childhoods and all that they experienced, while others won't feel any differently towards their childhood either way. Then others see their childhoods as a negative experience and blame everything they don't like about their lives on their parents.

Are you one of those who blame? Could it be that you didn't get what you needed as a child? And now, as an adult, do you find yourself in difficult situations or behaving in ways you don't understand? You may find yourself repeating scenarios that cause you hurt. Perhaps you might not know how to love because you were never shown love.

It is crucial to try and recognise what conditioning and patterns the past created in you if you are to understand why things in your life happen the way they do.

Unfortunately, some people's experiences contributed to childhoods that no child should have to go through. And because of confusing childhoods, they just can't figure things out as they get older. Perhaps you are someone who has experienced something that is nearly impossible to forgive and forget. Believe me, I see, feel, and hear your pain. The most natural thing for you to do is to want to hurt those who harmed you and make them suffer also. But if you continue to remain angry and unforgiving, you become a prisoner to your own mind and life.

Your biggest challenge is to forgive those who caused you trauma. If you are one of those people who was hurt and is still angry, just by picking up this book and deciding to read it, you are showing how strong, loving and forgiving you truly are and that you do want change. You know there is a better way to live.

Responsibility for Life

However, it may be that your hurt self wants to keep you blaming and feeling hurt. Maybe you like the little voice in your head that keeps telling you your problems today are everyone else's doing.

Everyone is responsible for their own lives—and yes, even when we think we have done nothing wrong in situations. You may disagree by thinking, 'But Michelle, you haven't felt the hurt and pain I went through. I was only a child; my parents were the adults who should have known better. I would never do what they did to anyone, let alone my own children.' What you believe is justified in every way to you.

But we cannot control what others do. We can only control what we do. And how we choose to respond to our pasts will either free us or keep us attached to our stories and heartache. If you continue wanting to be justified by your pain, then do so, but this will only keep you repeating patterns of behaviours that do not serve you.

Everything you have been taught and are doing—like getting angry, getting even, blaming, being a victim—is the opposite of what you need to do. Your brain convinces you that holding onto the old feelings of hurt and pain from the past offers you protection and keeps you safe. But it does not. There is no protection. In fact, all you are doing is causing yourself more hurt.

Taking responsibility, forgiving, and offering understanding, kindness, love, and support to every past situation is how you move away from them. It is easier said than done, though—I know. But even if you can't offer such a healing perspective to the past because you might not be ready, remaining neutral and unattached to what happened is better than having negative thoughts and feelings.

Negativity

No matter how hurtful, a negative view of any experience will keep us stuck and prevent us from moving on. The best way to change our present life is by forgiving those we think negatively contributed to our childhood. Begin to understand that your parents, or other people who had an influence on your upbringing, were just like you and not given a manual on life. Almost all they knew was what they learnt from their parents. They have their own conditioning. How can anyone be blamed if beliefs, thoughts, behaviours, wealth, and poverty have all been passed on through generations?

Evolvement

It's up to us to change what doesn't feel right to us between our generation and the next. This is evolvement. We all have made mistakes. We all have our own stories, and sometimes we need to be more compassionate and understanding towards everyone else's story. By forgiving the mistakes of previous generations or others, we allow them to forgive ours.

Suppose you end up getting things wrong with your own children. Wouldn't you want their forgiveness if you unintentionally hurt them? Of course, you would. Even if you don't have children, there is always someone in your life whose forgiveness you will want and need at some point in your life.

So often, our stories are not always what they seem to be. Do you need to revisit your story and change your perspective on it? Does it need some editing? Remember, you are the one who is relaying these stories, as these are your beliefs. How do you want to be seen? Reframe the story to how you want it to be. First, write it down, visualise it, and then verbalise and act it out in a way that leaves you feeling uplifted and empowered.

Everyone on this earth is at some level of Evolved Mental Maturity. To progress in your Evolved Mental Maturity is to accept past experiences for what they were at the time. This allows you to understand that everyone tried their best. Even if you felt hurt or unsupported, they probably didn't know they were causing the hurt, and it was undoubtedly not deliberate.

Above all, our pasts do not reflect who we are. Because of our evolvement, no defining moment in our lives, especially from childhood, governs who we are today.

Chapter 9
School and Society Create Beliefs

Learning occurs not only in the home but in school and society. School life plays a big part in our lives. Our experiences during those years can impact so many of our decisions throughout our lives.

First, school systems function by placing children into classes, then later on, putting them into sets. If someone is not considered 'normal', which is defined as being average in their ability to learn academically, they may be branded and grouped in certain categories called sets. The higher sets are for those who can achieve above-average results.

Labels

The problem with this system is that it applies labels to a child that can contribute to defining who they will think they are. They may grow up believing they are whatever the label says they are. As said in the previous chapter, every single one of us is different, which means we all learn in different ways. What can work for one student does not mean it can work for all.

I have experienced this with my own daughter. When we chatted about school, she would often talk about the higher, more able, Maths group. At ten-years-old, she had already been told she belonged in a category lower than the rest. Unfortunately, this could have led her to believe that she is not smart enough, that she is inadequate.

Every child knows exactly what is going on in school. It doesn't help them to see that other children get special treatment by going to a 'special' class because the school system labels them as 'more advanced'. Since this is accepted in society and no one speaks up about it, children may not be too bothered by this. However, how can we know the subtle psychological impact this may have on human beings?

It may seem reasonable and understandable to many why children are grouped into certain sets. But when children come home and have conversations about this sort of system, I have not come across a single child who explains that they are in a lower set because they are extremely smart. This is a form of subtle negative labelling that is unconsciously accepted so that it can contribute to someone developing a negative thought process about themselves growing up.

Society's Focus on 'Ability'

The school years are just the start of how we become conditioned to believe certain things about ourselves. The society and culture we are part of heaps many preconceptions on us, telling us what we need to have or achieve.

One such concept is the word *ability* when it is used to mean that someone does not have a specific ingredient to be something, achieve something, or move forward—instead of being a positive, it can be used as a negative—'the lack of'. Society encourages the belief that people need certain qualities, skills, or attributes to achieve and that we may not have achieved at something because we lacked some kind of ability.

Many think, were made to feel or may even have been told that they cannot pursue what they really want because they don't have the ability. For example, you may have failed Maths at school, but your dream has been to become a Maths teacher. So, you are left feeling that your dream of becoming a teacher is not achievable. In essence, society told you at some point in your life that you were not allowed to pursue something because you didn't fit into the general mould or have the requirements considered necessary to achieve something. Another example is if you were told at school, 'Because of your attitude, you will never make anything of your life.'

These messages become internalized as negative beliefs. It can be seen how this works when people make negative statements about themselves, such as: 'I was not very good at Drama, so I could never go into Theatre. I was told that I didn't have the ability for what it takes to become an athlete. I don't have the natural ability to understand science, so I can't be a doctor.' Internalized or conditioned messaging also creep into general negativity about ourselves in other areas, such as in statements like we have all said, 'I can never lose weight because I am not very good at exercising', or 'I am shy, so I can't communicate very well.'

The concept that certain abilities are required to achieve something and the negative labels we have come to believe about ourselves are very limiting.

Crippling Beliefs

The subtle beliefs we have taken in or created can impact how we see ourselves and our self-worth and could cripple us to the point that we can't do what we might want to do. Because of society's emphasis on the idea of 'ability' in order to achieve, often all other explanations and beliefs about life are not taught or explained to young adults. And this just leaves someone with the beliefs that cripple them.

We forget to explain that, even if you had failed Maths in school, it does not necessarily mean that you must give up on your dream or career hopes of becoming a Maths teacher. Sometimes, your wants and dreams come to pass in different ways.

We fail to tell students that their difficulty with Maths may not have been about them at all. It may have been because the method of education they received was not a fit for them or the environment was not good for them. It may have been that some of the teachers were acting out of their conditioning and couldn't relate to or provide them with what they needed at the time.

All of this might be why you could not comfortably learn. We also don't talk about how it could very well just click for you at some other point in life. You may need to go through some life experiences first, like learning about yourself, travelling, and maybe even experiencing what it's like to let go of a hurtful situation. It may be you needed to find yourself in another country, ten years after school, taking a course to be a Maths teacher to vulnerable children who need you more. Maybe you needed a certain level of knowledge and maturity to do this, and you might not have had that when you were young.

Wanting to Be a Writer

Leaving school, English was one of the subjects I least enjoyed. I found it extremely mundane and boring. There was no way I was going to entertain a career field in anything relating to English. I also didn't read very much as a child. I only started to enjoy reading in my twenties when I became a full-time reader. Writing a book was the last thing that I envisioned myself doing. But here I am years later, and my journey has brought me to this point of doing something where I should question my 'ability'.

Do I not pursue my desire to write this book just because I don't have the tools society says an accomplished writer must have? A quick Google search on 'What do I need to have to be a writer?' revealed the following steps someone can take to become a writer.

1. Earn a high school degree.
2. Select a professional path.
3. Get a writing education.
4. Complete an internship.
5. Land a job and build a portfolio.
6. Earn an MA/MFA.

At first glance, this did not fill me with the utmost confidence. I didn't find many encouraging articles that really pushed me to proceed. I could accept defeat and believe I don't have what it takes to try. My writing might be criticised by someone who feels they can do a better job. But in reality, my words and the experience I share are just as effective or meaningful whether I have a high school degree or a writing education or not. We can all pick holes in what people do because we think their skill set isn't as good as ours.

Deep Knowing

Parents and other adults may have thought they were only trying to do what's best for you. Yet, someone else's view or experience may be totally different to yours. You may have a deep feeling or 'knowing' about something you need to be doing. I am sure you have heard the phrase, 'I feel it in my gut.' This is your intuition. Your intuition is only positive. It is there to help and guide you. When your gut speaks, you should not go against it. You feel this way for a reason, so do not question it when it regards something positive—go ahead and change it. Change what feels right for you.

Different Ways to Achieve a Dream

There can be ways to achieve your dreams that are not limited to a certain ability. This isn't saying that someone can decide to become an athlete from one day to the next. You didn't learn to walk and ride a bike by only doing it once, nor were you limited to one try to learn them. There are steps in every process in life, steps that anyone can follow, but at times you may be unable to see them. The way you learn is to put in the effort and consistently try.

So, all these limiting beliefs we have about ourselves concerning what we can't do—because that's what school, society or someone told us—are incorrect. There may be other paths that could still lead you to achieve your dreams. Take, for instance, being a professional singer. Some singers are highly successful and have had hit after hit despite never having attended music school or received professional training, except for having only taken some singing classes. Then you have someone who has spent years of vocal and music training in a conventional system that society accepts as the path to achieving in this profession—yet who ends up not having a successful career.

Of course, there are always skills that can be gained or improved in any field, but sometimes we think we need to be totally professionally trained and skilled up to do something we wish to do. And such a belief prevents us from pursuing it because we feel inadequate.

We all have ability. No one is born with extra special powers, and we need to accept that we might have convinced ourselves there is no way. Similarly, we should never close off what we truly want or convince ourselves that it's not for us when we have tried but may have failed to achieve it. Just because something didn't work for you the first time does not mean it never will. You are enough and have all the abilities to do exactly what it is you want. **If you wholeheartedly believe something is for you, it's time to believe it is.**

Becoming Good at Something

More often than not, we become very good at something because we

1. Actually believe we can

2. Make a start, even if we have doubts or don't know where to begin

3. Consistently work at it

Over time this approach accumulates into experience and then mastery in a field you never thought you could do.

Of course, this approach does not deny the years an expert will put into studying a subject at university or college to obtain their knowledge of their subject. But more often than not, the expert's truest knowledge comes from their real-life experience.

Much of the time, we are able to gain experience and become good at something simply because we have come to believe that we can do it. This is because we have not limited ourselves by thinking there is only one way to achieve something. Suppose we attend the workshop of someone who has been in and out of prison ten times, did not have 'ability' at school nor has higher education, but is now a multimillionaire with personal growth and life experience to offer. We can also attend a workshop by someone with a university degree who has studied a subject for many years and is also a multi-millionaire. There are different paths, ways, and choices along the way. And because of this, two very different people can both be worthy and have the ability to provide you with the same message: 'Always go for what you want. And never give up.' Unfortunately, too many in the world remain focused on a labelling system to make things more achievable and acceptable for people to fit into.

So, reflect on whether you have ever experienced having labels put upon you and if you find yourself still using and believing those same labels. Think about what you think or have been told that you are 'able' to do. Observe where and how your beliefs have limited or continue to limit you.

A little exercise to help you work through your labels is to write down what you believe them to be. They should be placed under two headings: Labels That Are True About Me and Labels Others Imposed On Me. Once you have done this, go through each one and ask, Does this label serve me in my life right now? Sometimes our labels have served us at one point in our lives. If they still do, then great, but if they do not, how can the narrative be changed on this? How can I improve on this? What support and action do I need to take?

Now accept that you are born into systems that may have contributed to how you see yourself. But know there is no right or wrong way of learning, no quicker or slower, no dumber or cleverer. There is no such thing as high achievers or low achievers. We *all* have the potential to achieve anything we want because, in the end, we all have our own personal growth to explore.

People who are very accomplished aren't different from you. They didn't achieve so much because they had a better education or were born lucky. It's not because they are secret superheroes. They just wholeheartedly believed they could do what they set out to do, and as they did, they faced all their obstacles.

Chapter 10
Learning from Parenting

We Can Learn from Children

The previous chapters showed how conditioned we can become in childhood and how school and society can give us negative beliefs about ourselves. For many of us, our childhood is a distant memory, and we spend most of our teenage years wishing to be an adult. Later, we spend the time reminiscing about how easy and carefree being young was before life presented its challenges and responsibilities. This is one of the many cycles of life.

Suppose you don't want to Self-Reflect about your past too much. It wasn't so bad for you, and there is plenty to worry about today as a parent yourself. If this is the case, there is no doubt that you will be given many important lessons to help you grow and evolve as a parent.

If we pay attention, we can learn so much from the children around us, even though we sometimes allow life's challenges to cloud our awareness. For one thing, we can remember that we were once children too. This means we had the very same qualities children possess before we allowed our habits and behaviours to become complicated and forgot what is important in life—being kind and happy, giving and receiving unconditional love, and living a life with purpose.

Children don't carry any hate; there is a light-heartedness to them. Children can play games with one another though they sometimes fall into disagreements. A child might get upset and tell an adult about what has happened. Once the adult sorts out the problem, the child sees it as confirmation that the adult is letting the other child know what they did upset them. They do this because children have not yet learnt the art of communicating with one another. Once the adult has said something to sort the situation out, the child will go off and play as though nothing has happened. They can do this because children do not hold on to resentment, anger or hate. They do not decide to stop speaking or playing with the other child again (like adults tend to do).

We, as adults, hold on to things when there is no need to. We are the ones who say, 'I am never speaking to that person again; they hurt me, they upset me.' There is certainly some irony in it all. We can remember who we as children were before we learnt all the added things that do not serve us.

Learning from Parenting

If watching children can teach us valuable lessons, then how we parent or interact with them can be an even greater opportunity for growth. We offer many teachings to children, but an important one is how we set the example. How we deal with situations can influence and mould children into whom they become.

Things can become exhausting when you are trying to juggle life and its demands, all while still being an example to your children. You are still figuring yourself out and do have really tough days at times. You get tired, make mistakes and misread situations. Because of the internal and external pressure you are under, sometimes you take your mood out on them, unable to realise the impact we could be having on impressionable children.

Everyone sometimes makes mistakes and gets parenting wrong, but many seldom take responsibility for their part. For example, you arrive home after a really stressful day at work. Your child is not doing anything particularly different from what they would normally do, but your tolerance on that day is less than what it would be. The child says one thing that really annoys you, and you can't control yourself and lash out at the child. Later, upon reflection, you know you acted out, but you leave the child thinking and believing they misbehaved by back chatting.

In this scenario, most of us do not pause for a second and apologise to the child. We often leave it and think that it has probably not affected them in any way. We ignore that we know we were wrong or tell ourselves we'll behave differently the next time. However, this leaves the child feeling and believing that they did wrong and were naughty. In fact, it was we who were having a bad day and couldn't get a handle on our emotions.

Have an open dialogue with your children. Address what occurred, the feelings and your reaction. Admit when you are unable to figure out your own emotions. If you set the example, show vulnerability and apologise for your mistakes, children can see that we do get things wrong while still being their parent. When you show them that you are not perfect but can take responsibility for the things you do, you are teaching them Self-Reflection.

In the previous chapters, I spoke about letting go of our upbringings and conditioning if these don't serve us. Still, there are behaviour patterns that remain part of who we are. This is why it is not always easy finding the correct balance between allowing children to express themselves freely and teaching them. Because we sometimes do not know we practice old behaviours, we may still inflict fear or model behaviours that will not serve them when they grow up.

Situations you experienced when you were young can still influence what you do, especially with children. Part of your journey as a parent is to recognise the behaviours you display that do not serve you.

Doing What Benefits Our Status

Another thing we can find ourselves doing as parents is to do, subconsciously, what would secretly benefit our status. Sometimes, we can push our dreams onto our children and convince ourselves we are doing it for them. But the real reason behind encouraging our children to follow certain dreams could be that it is a dream or vision that we have so longed to do but never achieved. It may even be something our parents stopped us from pursuing, so now we feel it is too late for us.

Selfishly, you may want to be able to brag that your child is a doctor because this is what you think will look good to others. Or suppose your child wants to be an artist, but you don't view this as a career of any substance, so you disregard their dream. Instead of encouraging it, you convince them to do something else. If you realise that you are parenting based on your unlived dreams or what will help your status, it's never too late to change who you are as a parent. Deep down, no one wants to make their children feel unhappy.

Sometimes our job as parents is to stand by and allow children to make decisions for themselves and allow them to learn on their own path. Sometimes just being there without judgement is all the support they need. We may see things very differently from our children, which is OK—that's what makes us all unique.

Love and support contribute to happiness, while being forced into something we don't necessarily want to do only builds disappointment and resentment. We and our children, all of us, will find ourselves eventually in a position to help the natural progression of the evolvement of life for the greater good.

Watching What You Say

If you look around, everything you see comes from a thought, and thoughts are words. It is especially important to listen to, observe, and reflect on the words that do leave your mouth. Many of the answers to your questions are in what you say.

Another example of our responsibility as adults is watching what we say around children. The way we speak and the words we use are probably just like what you heard spoken in the household where you grew up.

But many of the words and phrases we use are often associated with negativity, and without realising it, we are inflicting limitations upon ourselves and the children around us. We use phrases like: 'No, don't do that. Just shut up; you're doing my head in. You're not allowed to do that. Do it, you silly child. You shouldn't do that; what are people going to say? Stop acting that way. You are being an idiot. Stop acting like that. You are an embarrassment to the family!'

In addition to how we speak to children, they hear us use our words in talking about others. The words we use have the impact to be immensely powerful and leave their imprint on us and others. Children don't have the capacity to know the context of our words. Their brains are not developed yet, so they can't differentiate between jokes, innuendo, or sarcasm. They don't know what to dismiss. A child views any words and phrases it has learnt as either good or bad. Speaking negatively and judging others teaches children that it is acceptable to behave this way.

The Naughty Step

A while ago, I watched a programme on TV about someone who went into people's homes to help parents deal with their misbehaving children. One method used was if a child was naughty, they were sent to an allocated area in the house, such as a chair, step or mat, which was called the naughty step. They had to sit there alone for an allocated time, depending on their age. It did appear to work.

So, after watching the programme, I decided that I was going to try this method with my own children. Whenever I thought they were 'naughty', they were sent to the naughty step. After doing this for some time, one day, my son did something 'naughty'. I can't remember exactly what he did, but I remember getting very upset and telling him off. When I told him that he was naughty because of what he had done and he was going to be taken to the naughty step, he turned to me and was very upset. Tears welled up in his eyes as he said, 'Mommy, *I didn't know that was going to happen.*' These were very powerful words, and they took me aback. It almost felt like a light bulb moment, but with it also came feelings of pain and regret for the hurt I had caused my son.

My son had done something not because he was 'bad' but because he genuinely did not understand that what he had done would cause the result it did. Yet, I was going to set him apart once again to question himself as a person and think that I felt he was bad and that I didn't love him. Any child that is sent away and excluded because of their behaviour can't help but feel sad.

If we look at synonyms for the word *naughty*, they are: *disobedient, bad, mischievous* and *badly behaved*. To think we use this word so mindlessly. I stopped sending my children to the naughty step and decided all those years ago that using the word 'naughty' was one small change I was going to make. And I also tried very hard not to use certain words with negative connotations about my children's experiences.

Furthermore, based on my experience, I don't believe children are 'naughty' in any way. They just don't always know how to act. Children will often behave in a way that imitates their parents or the adults around them. Children are inexperienced in navigating life and need help and guidance from parents to do so.

When my children seriously played up because they had very little experience of a situation and didn't understand the impact of their choices, I would instead explain to them to have a 'thinking time'. I would ask them to think about what had happened and to determine whether they thought it had a negative or positive feeling. Then we would talk, and I'd ask whether they felt their choice was misguided or resulted in something they had not expected to happen. We would also discuss what to do if they found themselves in the same or a similar situation and if they could try doing the opposite. Could there be a kinder way to act if they weren't being kind? And how would they feel if it had been done to them?

What this did was allow us to have open communication. Speaking openly about how we felt about certain things and situations became OK. It was an opportunity for Self-Reflection. Communication became second nature to us, so we were able to recognise feelings of anger, hurt, frustration, confusion and the possible reasons why we could be feeling those ways. We did not get it right all the time, but for the most part, we did.

The next chapter further discusses the power of words, thoughts, and labels as it applies to you and your conditioning.

Chapter 11
Self-Identifying Thoughts

When we were growing up, our parents, teachers and other adults used words toward and about us without realising their power and impact. Suppose you were regularly told you were 'bad' when, just like my son in the example in the previous chapter, you were not 'bad'. You just did not know what the outcome of your actions would be. You did not intend to cause harm; you were just inexperienced.

Words used over and over about someone can lead them to feel a certain way and form thoughts about themselves. They identify with the labels that end up creating someone's self-identity.

Such self-identifying thoughts can also be our beliefs about who we are and what we may feel about the past—like our needs weren't met or we are not entitled to anything. If we believe we weren't shown love, we can identify as someone who never receives love and is unable to show love to others or ourselves.

As we grow up and form mature identities, labels become part of it. In addition to negative self-identifying labelling, we also carry positive thoughts about ourselves, which form our identities as well.

Words Surround Us

From babyhood onward, we constantly hear words spoken around us. Words arise and float in our heads every second of the day and roll off our tongues without much thought. Words are broken-down narratives of our thoughts and feelings. We use words to describe situations, others and ourselves. But we also use words to label ourselves just as the systems we are part of do, just as our parents did without realising it.

In addition to our ingrained self-identifying thoughts, we use labels all the time to define who we are. We identify ourselves by our professions, like calling ourselves a nurse, a teacher or a driver, and we also identify ourselves by roles such as wife, daughter, or husband.

There was a time when I described myself as someone who was mischievous when I was young. I described myself this way because it is what I was made to think and feel. I have always been a fairly confident person, so this self-identifying thought about myself did not stop me too much. Deep down, I didn't truly believe that I was mischievous. I believed I was a young person who was just curious. I loved life and wanted to experience as much of it as possible. But if I had been someone who did not feel positively about myself this way, the label might have had quite a different effect.

How Do You Speak About Yourself and Others?

Suppose you were to step outside of yourself and listen to yourself speaking. What would you hear? Are your words always negative? Or do you always speak kindly about yourself and others? Do you find yourself saying things like, 'Oh, I am not very good at that, I can't do that. I am not smart enough. I do not have enough money; if I did, my life would be different.'?

There are many, many words that we place on ourselves and that have been placed on us. 'Mischievous' is only one example to explain the impact of using words to label ourselves. Other examples are stupid, clumsy, greedy, bully, and bossy. All these words could leave lasting effects on anyone if used repeatedly, let alone on impressionable children. Without being conscious, you can very easily speak negatively about yourself, even in a joking or serious way on a daily basis.

We should always try to speak positively about anyone in any situation. Words are powerful and can affect children and us for many years—all the no's, shouldn't's, couldn't's, and name calling. If we could manage to correct and change how we speak to others and ourselves from, 'No, you can't' to 'OK, why don't you give it a try', we would be shifting our lives into forward action. If we change what we say and rephrase how we speak to our children, to one another, and most importantly, to ourselves, we will get better outcomes in our lives.

We also use our words to judge others. At some point, everyone has sat around watching a TV programme and negatively commented out loud about the people on the show. We may note how badly they are dressed, how annoying they are, and how ugly or fat they are. And we do this with impressionable, young children around. It is a behavioural pattern many of us were exposed to ourselves and learnt in the home as it is passed down from generation to generation absent-mindedly. We have been taught and have taught to judge.

Most times, when we feel the need to comment on others in a negative way, it's because we are not happy with something within ourselves. We may feel insecure or inadequate compared to other people. We might think they are smarter than us or prettier than us, and because of this, putting them down makes us feel better about ourselves at that moment. But it doesn't take away those feelings we have about ourselves.

The negative thoughts or statements about others won't go away until you find out and correct what is missing within yourself. Spend time reflecting on whether the way you speak about yourself and others is the authentic you. Observe yourself in conversation. How much of it consists of talking about other people and judging them? Study your own thinking. How much of it is about self-identifying thoughts and labels? Do these need to be changed?

Can You Change Your Thoughts to Change Your Life?

There is an old adage that states, 'If you change your thoughts, you can change your life.' Sounds pretty simple, doesn't it? But if this basic concept works, why are we not changing our lives? It sounds as if changing our thoughts is such an easy thing to do. Since most of us do want to live a better life, why aren't we? People have told me that they have changed their thoughts, but it didn't work because nothing changed, no matter how hard they tried.

Samantha, a young lady I once knew, was someone who came across that very idea after reading about it in a magazine article. She told me about her situation. One of the things she wanted to change was being unfit. Samantha understood that if she wanted to get fitter, she would need to exercise. Through her Self-Reflection, she believed her limiting thoughts about exercise were that she didn't have the time to exercise. She said she was far too busy with work and family life to fit it in.

At that point, Samantha decided to change her thinking to, 'I do have time.' She repeated this daily. Upon waking up and before going to sleep, she would repeat, 'I do have time. I want to get fitter. I have time to exercise and be fitter. I will get fitter.' She believed that, after some time doing this practice, it had started to form a shift within her. She started to feel motivated and got out her colourful pens and new diary. She took the time to write up a rota and pencilled in 30-minute walks every second day for the next two weeks. Samantha felt good about this. She believed she had managed to change her thoughts.

The day before Samantha was going to start incorporating her new action—which stemmed from her new thought process—she met some of her friends for lunch. One of them was very much into fitness, and they got on the subject of exercising. Samantha mentioned that the following day she was going to go on a walk as she had read that it was a great form of exercise. Her friend suggested that Samantha would benefit from doing some jogging. Samantha instantly laughed and told her friend that she couldn't possibly do any jogging because she was not very good at it. In fact, she was not good at any sports. Her friend argued that everyone could jog. But Samantha told her that, when she was young, she was the slowest in her class and would dread sports day or any competitive sports at school. Her friends laughed at her because she always came in last at everything. She was called 'Snail Samantha'. Samantha told this story as a joke, brushing away any sort of seriousness.

Samantha's walks never lasted very long, and on the days when she was due to go on them, by mid-morning, she had already convinced herself there was something much more important she needed to do instead. She couldn't keep to any sort of exercise schedule and always found excuses.

Over the years, we have undergone thousands of experiences, all stored in our subconscious minds and deeply rooted in our brains. If we can't recognise our real thoughts about something, how can we change our thoughts to change our lives?

Sometimes we can't always recall the exact moment a past hurt has come from. Samantha was able to recall the hurtful incident from when she was young, but she didn't think that it was the real reason she didn't exercise. Instead, she convinced herself it was because she didn't have the time.

Samantha thought of herself as emotionally stable and confident within herself, so how could something so trivial affect her? But it had. She had allowed words like 'Snail Samantha' to label her. She self-identified as someone who was not very good at something, and because of this, she did not see an alternative. She allowed a self-identifying thought to create a negative belief about herself.

She also made an association of needing speed to be able to run because of always coming in last. Your brain can develop a false association to something, and these associations can become muddled as to what the actual reality is based on your emotions. Samantha certainly needed to get over the hurt of being called 'Snail Samantha'.

In Samantha's case, because she was confident about who she is, she didn't make the connection that her experience as a child had impacted her choices about exercise. It was going on subconsciously and covered up as she made excuses.

Addressing Old Wounds

Like many of us, Samantha may need to address a past hurt. Once Samantha lets go of her childhood experience and limiting beliefs, she will be able to remove any blockages she has. Of course, she can exercise and jog—you do not need any speed to do it. This is why changing your thoughts to change your life is not done by just repeating words. Your brain has been embedded with a way of learning.

It is possible to change your thoughts, but it can be very difficult to change if you don't understand what you self-identify as first. Especially since some part of it could be associated with any conditioning you received growing up.

We limit ourselves by what we have come to identify ourselves with. So, to truly 'change your thoughts to change your life', uncover all the self-identifying labels that do not serve you. Most of the answers to uncovering how you truly feel about yourself are in the words you say. Refrain from labelling yourself even in jokes, sarcasm, or innuendos because your brain can't differentiate between these things. If you consistently work on changing these labels, you will overcome all the limitations you inflict on yourself over time.

Chapter 12
Conditioned Expectations

We all have many dreams, goals, and aspirations. We may have envisioned these wants in great detail and expected things to unfold exactly how we had visualized them. But when what we hope for doesn't turn out the way we planned, it can leave us feeling hurt and disappointed.

If your expectations never seem to come to fruition, do you just forget about your dreams and goals to avoid being further disappointed and let down? Nobody wants to keep feeling like a failure, especially after continuously investing time and energy into dreams and goals. But how can you grow, change, or achieve if you don't allow yourself any expectations? Sometimes what we work for doesn't succeed simply because it wasn't what we truly wanted from our authentic selves in the first place.

False Acceptance

We are meant to have dreams and expectations, but some of our hoped-for desires are not always our own. What does this mean? There are a few contributing factors that play a part in influencing our expectations. These are the systems we are born into, our upbringing and society. We are surrounded by many stereotypes and preconceptions of what life is meant to be like. The most common stereotypes are cultural, social, racial, gender-based, and religious.

An example of one common stereotype that has been around for centuries (though it is slowly changing) is what young boys should grow up to be. They are expected to become strong and tough and be the providers of the household as the head of the family. Meanwhile, even today, young girls are expected to have children, be responsible for the home's upkeep, and look after the family when they grow up. Another example of a stereotype regards education. If someone has obtained a higher education, they may be considered to be of superior intellect and importance. Having a degree may cause others to see someone as being of higher status, particularly if their profession is being a judge, doctor, or solicitor.

The stereotypes impressed on us by our upbringing or society can influence us to believe that we must strive to do certain things or create specific circumstances in our lives to be accepted in this world. And without realizing it, we might end up working towards goals we didn't necessarily want and weren't right for us just because we believed it was something we had to do.

The adults around you growing up were also exposed to this type of influence, and because of this, they may have unconsciously projected their dreams and desires upon you. An example of this is when someone was raised in a household where both their parents were solicitors, and the expectation was that the child would follow in the family's footsteps. This idea was subtly drilled into them from a young age. Initially, they don't reject this idea for their life because they do believe it's their desire to become a solicitor even though they had other interests growing up.

The person applies themselves and does all that is needed to get a law degree and become a solicitor. However, years later, they feel unfulfilled, sad and unhappy. Deep within, throughout the years, something kept nagging at them—a desire to do something else, something that their family or others would not widely accept. They also don't want to disappoint their parents and certainly don't want to be seen as a failure. When thinking about pursuing their desired dreams, thoughts of fear and doubt fill their minds.

When we've taken on the expectations of others in our lives, we can become confused and feel unfulfilled. We feel like this because we can't understand that it was never our own goals and desires that we were pursuing but someone else's projection. At times, many of us will go along blindly, wholeheartedly believing our goals and dreams are the things we authentically want. Just because it was your parents' and their parents' paths to become solicitors or butchers or to run the family business doesn't mean it is yours. Maybe they chose their professions for the right reasons, but further down the line, when it came to their children following them, it became about security and status.

Partnership

Today there are many different types of romantic and committed relationships between people. Some choose not to marry but to live together. Others never marry. And we have same-sex marriage now.
Marriage/partnership is another huge area where conditioned expectations can exist. Even today, the idea that someone should find a particular, 'suitable' type of partner, get married and have children is imposed on many as they grow up.

Suppose you did as was expected of you. You found someone who would fit well into your family and look good from a societal perspective, so you married. Yet, years later, you find that you don't relate to your spouse and are facing a decision that goes against what is 'accepted' in society and your family. Do you let everyone down, be a failure, and end up just another divorcee?

Unfortunately, getting married, staying together and living happily ever after is a conditioned expectation, just as the idea that the end of a marriage is a failure. Marriage may have been an experience meant for you, but the type of person you were raised to believe you needed was not. Later on, when you realise that your marriage partner was all wrong for you, you may be left feeling that you don't deserve to be happy because you made the wrong choice—even when others actually dictated this choice.

Understanding

It might seem very hard to understand why your expectations don't unfold as you had hoped. But understanding will come as you Self-Reflect, observe, and tap into the authenticity of who you are. You may come to see that just like how some of your behaviours and reactions were passed down to you from prior generations, so too were family expectations. Your original dreams may not have been your true goals and desires but conditioned expectations that were imprinted on you.

It is OK to realise that that old dream of yours that you once so desperately wanted is not good for you. Your conditioned learning has led you to do certain things, but these things are not the path you are meant to continue on, and over time you will come to know this when things just don't feel right for you anymore.

When you go through hurtful experiences and disappointment about your choices, you will come out the other side, look back, and realise that what you went through was for the best. You will come to understand the saying, 'What you think you want is not necessarily what you need.'

Here is a quote of mine that speaks to the heart of our very existence: **Never give up on your hopes, dreams,** and desires; just surrender and let go of a definite outcome.

You always get what you wish for but just don't realise it. It can manifest in many ways, so hold true to exactly what you want. Know, though, that it comes in ways that your mind has not yet imagined.

Chapter 13
Social Media and the Consumers Market

Image

Have you ever woken up, not brushed your hair, put on your tackiest clothing, basically given very little attention to your appearance, and then attended a social gathering? Probably not. For some time now, the common view is that we have to look, dress, and act a certain way to be accepted. Image is all-important, even if real self-love and self-care are almost nonexistent.

We can put tremendous pressure on ourselves to seem acceptable in society. Striving to obtain the perfect image of how we and our lives are meant to look may leave us experiencing feelings of anxiety, low self-esteem, worthlessness, and unhappiness. Why do we build an image of having a perfect body, perfect house, perfect car, and perfect children and family? Some push themselves to have all that to the point of losing who they are because they believe it will make them happy. All image chasing does is make them very unhappy and feel unworthy because there is no such thing as perfection.

Media

Unfortunately, more than ever, we are part of societal systems that lead us to believe we need to project certain images. Social segregation in cultures has always been around, but with the evolution of technology, we find ourselves at a stage where there is widespread negativity amongst people because of social media and the images it imposes.

Technology *is* wonderful. It can make us feel close to loved ones, even if they live on the other side of the world. But like everything in life, social media has both advantages and disadvantages with the potential to have either positive or negative effects on us. If we are already struggling with self-esteem and self-identifying labels, then having the extra pressure of seeing everyone else's 'perfect lives' does not help. We all need to be a little more mindful about what we are exposed to and how we use or react to what's on the Internet.

Marketing

Unfortunately, the concept of being perfect is associated—a lot of the time—with materialistic things. We are all in a huge consumer market part of a massive profits game.

For example, the market tells us that if we buy a product, it will make us happy. It can be the simplest thing, something that we don't even need. But with the correct marketing tools, a company can make us feel we must have it. Some companies hire psychologists to work with their marketing teams. Because they understand human behaviour, they know exactly what to do to convince consumers they really need a product when they don't. The truth of the matter is they play to our wants, needs, and emotions. And we are made to feel our desire is our decision. Of course, it is great to have nice things. Everyone can appreciate a bit of luxury. Who wouldn't enjoy taking a boat ride on 'the crystal blue waters of the Mediterranean Sea' with no expense spared or a top-of-the-range car that provides smooth driving?

But the messaging can also trigger our insecurities and so negatively affect our well-being. Half the time, we do not know this is happening to us. So, the question is, at what point do we stop allowing social media and marketing to trigger our insecurities?

Something to Buy Happiness

All of us, at some point in our lives, have thought that buying a certain item would contribute to making us happy or help us get what we want. Through consumer marketing and social media, we are influenced to believe that buying certain things will help push us to obtain our perfect lives.

It can play out in many ways. Suppose someone desperately wants to find a partner but thinks they need to lose some weight first. This idea is because every person they have come across (on social media) with a partner looks like they have a perfect body. Later they find a product online that promises to enable weight loss without hard work. All that is required is taking a pill every day. The marketing assures them they will lose weight in no time by taking it. They take the pill for a week and even begin to eat relatively healthier.

Then a week later, the person finds themself on the sofa, binging on unhealthy food after an emotional day. Now they are experiencing feelings of failure and guilt. The binge continues, and the pills are of no use to them. It turns out that the very fine print of the product says that, for the product to truly work, the buyer has to eat a healthy diet too. Now, the buyer can't help to not only feel like a weight-loss failure but think, 'I will never find a partner because I am just too fat.'

In most cases, when you want to buy something or do something because you believe it will help make your life perfect, what is actually needed is that explore and discover what you really need. That is, not a bought 'magic pill' to lose weight, but to find out the real reason why you are not eating correctly in the first place or why you believe you have to have a perfect body to be worthy of love.

False Reality

A picture is worth a million words. And if we are not careful, we can interpret even a single photo on social media into a false story about reality and allow it to make us feel that we are not enough—because we are not living a glamorous life like others are.

Unfortunately, no one ever posts images of when they are feeling sad and lonely or the struggles they are going through.

Often, we can become confused, and our emotions get mixed up because we believe that the images being flashed in our faces every day are what we should aspire to. We become convinced that they represent what we need to be, and if we and our lives don't live up to or resemble what others have or are doing, then we are not enough.

So many of us have bought into a false reality of what women and men are supposed to look like physically. We believe we need to create an image of ourselves to look like we have flawless skin, a wrinkle-free face, big lips, buff muscles, and a six-pack. Young impressionable children think that this is reality.

Social media and consumer marketing create tremendous pressure to look like photoshopped and surgery-sculpted models when humans are not naturally like that. The natural body has stretch marks, lumps, rolls, laugh lines, scars, spots, and wrinkles. Moreover, everybody comes in different shapes and sizes. This, however, is not displayed in consumer marketing because, if it were, it would mean that it is acceptable to look like this. Then selling items to make you 'sexier', 'more beautiful', or 'thinner', give you an 'instant six pack', and 'get rid of wrinkles' wouldn't be such a lucrative market anymore. **As sad as it might sound, the** more insecurities people have about themselves, the better it is for profits.

If you find yourself always looking at images and thinking that you need to change who you are to become more like someone else, then that could be a sign that you are covering up some problem you don't want to face and sort out. Similarly, buying material things, at times, are attempts at quick fixes to a situation or problem. If you have to buy and have certain things to feel accepted by your peers or others, then there is some internal struggle that needs addressing as to why you might be feeling this way. Buying provides comfort for a short while. But we need to get to the real reason why we do what we do.

We fail to understand that even if we have a perfect body, perfect family, perfect job, and perfect children, we can still be very unhappy. Happiness must be obtained within ourselves, before the partner, children, and before the house. Our inner happiness and authenticity are what make these situations happy, not the other way around. We need to accept who we are, and that includes all the things you 'think' you don't like about yourself and the things you love about yourself.

Chapter 14
Understanding Fear

We have all heard the phrase, 'The innocence of a child.' It speaks to the carefree nature of children. You were an innocent and happy child at one point in your life. You were born without fear, but you were also born into a world with conditioning and systems that affected you. Now, like so many, your life may be governed by fear.

Growing up, you may have been raised in a religion or culture with certain beliefs or laws that undoubtedly influenced the way you think. Certain values do have an element of causing us to fear things, in part because our existence has a certain unknown quality. Often the conditioning and societal values that engender fear in us do not serve us. How can they if we all end up learning to fear?

Your Brain Believes It Needs to Keep You Safe from Threat

The human brain is very black and white in its signalling. It needs to be because of its complex functioning. Consider how amazing it is that we can walk and talk, take in oxygen as breath and have all our bodily functions working without us even knowing how.

What the brain has learnt to do, through no fault of its own, is believe it needs to keep us safe from any threat, including emotional threats.

Our brains cannot differentiate between what we were once told as a precaution against something that could have been potentially dangerous for our safety and survival and something that is no threat to us at all, apart from it being new. My brain cannot say, 'Hey Michelle, these feelings you are currently experiencing fall in the category of having a natural, healthy precaution', as opposed to, 'Hey Michelle, what you are feeling right now is made up. It is not related to anything bad happening. All this is something that I associated with something else because of suggestions made to me in my upbringing. It is a false belief that I have created along the way. You are not in danger.'

The brain cannot distinguish between something that deserves to be feared—natural fear—and a false association—man-made fear. No matter what fear you are confronting, when certain feelings tell you there is a potential threat, your brain will automatically try to protect you.

Natural Fear

But what is fear? Why do we fear, and how do we stop being fearful? We talk of it as if it is a living thing and give it tremendous power. Firstly, what needs to be understood is that there are two types of fear. The first one is real fear, which is associated with immediate danger.

Mankind learnt ways of dealing with natural fears. For instance, long ago, many people died from snake bites. Men began to fear these creatures because they caused death. So, when snakes appeared, people were cautious and took action to avoid them. Dealing with natural fears is instinctive for us. It can happen automatically in the same way we breathe and our hearts beat.

Another example of natural fear would be when you are walking down a dangerously steep rocky slope. Common sense would tell you not to run or rush down the slope. You would be very careful as you moved, being sure to place your feet solidly so as not to trip. The fear of tripping or falling down such a steep hill is real and natural. Your survival instinct gives you this fear. And by taking the necessary precautions to protect yourself, you can easily deal with this fear.

But every day, we also find ourselves dealing not only with natural fear. Humanity has evolved to the point where we have created fears that are false illusions: man-made fears.

Man-Made Fears

There are layers and layers to our minds. As discussed in earlier chapters, we all have a certain programming or conditioning that also contributes to determining our mindset or way of thinking. So we have the brain's natural functioning as it responds to fear together with the subconscious with its conditioning and experiences as well as our own personality and the traits we were born with that make us, us - all stored in our minds. Wow, that is a whole lot of functioning going on, all in that little head of ours that we never get to see.

Our man-made (MM) fears spring from our subconscious and conditioning—our limitations, labels and self-identifying thoughts. MM fears include not being good enough, failing, rejection, making the wrong decision, never finding love, and of being alone. MM fears arose every time we were taught to fear something or experienced a situation that frightened us. Whether there was a natural fear there or not, MM fears limit us because they can prevent us from taking action or moving forward. And like boundary walls, these fear-based limitations create our comfort zones (more on comfort zones in Chapter 18).

For example, suppose someone grew up around people who were overly cautious about everything they did. As that person develops into an adult, they may adopt a risk-averse approach to life without realising it.

Or suppose a child attends play centres that have loads of climbing apparatus, yet they are constantly being told, 'Do not climb on that, you will fall. Do not carry on jumping, or you will hurt yourself. Stop running around; you are going to run into someone.' In fact, the child who falls while playing may be told, 'You see, I told you, you would fall. Be careful. Just stop doing that now. You do not want it to happen again.' And because of the painful emotions like crying over the physical hurt from falling, you started to learn fears connected to running and playing.

These very normal spoken phrases that occur in our lives have contributed to our view of the world. Of course, we were being told these cautions to ensure our safety since our less-developed brains may not have been able to foresee danger or how something could pose a risk. But there may have been other things that we were learning and exploring that did not represent any kind of risk to us yet were still talked about by adults in a fearful way.

Here is an example. When you grew up, your mum may have been a bit fed up, she might have been having a bad day, and you were jumping around in the garden. You wanted to play hopscotch. Even though you had played hopscotch many times before, because you once fell and grazed your knee while playing, your mum said you couldn't play anymore because you would hurt yourself again. Instead of your mum identifying and recognising that she was, in fact, grumpy and feeling impatient that day, she used fear to persuade you not to do something.

How real are man-made fears? MM fear can be very real. It can stop us from doing something we would like to do. It can even go so far as to paralyse us physically.

But how can we tackle this fear when it can feel like we have no control over it and that it controls us?

To tackle an MM fear, we need to understand where it could have possibly originated and then change the association we have made to it that enabled it to become a fear in the first place. Fear originates from thought, and our thoughts generate feelings of fear.

Which Identifications Are Being Triggered?

Reactions based on fear derive from a whole bunch of negative thoughts and feelings that tell us something bad can happen again. These reactions create a lot of self-doubt in us. Some of what we fear is also linked to our self-identifying labels. As previously discussed, slowly, over time in life, most of us adopt and apply labels to ourselves and others as we describe ourselves and others in a certain way.

Take, for example, if someone has a self-identifying belief that they are kind and were often liked by others growing up. What happens when they face a scenario where people don't see them that way or even like them, like at a social club? They could start to fear going to the club because of how invested they are in the identification of being liked. It's as if the self-identifying label feels under attack.

On the other hand, sometimes, our self-identifications stand strong against life's currents. Say a person identifies themselves as being extremely smart. In this case, the person would probably not associate anything that questioned their intelligence with fear because their belief that their intellect can tackle anything is so strong.

So, when you are reacting with fear to certain situations or challenges in life, you need to ask yourself, what self-identifications are being triggered? The stronger your associations with self-identifying thoughts, beliefs, and values, the stronger the fear can be. When we start to fear doing things in life, it is because we have made it about our self-image instead of the real reason we wanted to do it in the first place.

Being Stuck

There are certain things we set out to do in life, but at times, we get stuck because we are scared. We get excited about something, imagining the possibilities of what could develop, and then we stop and think about all the things that could go wrong, and we are filled with dread.

Suppose it was someone's goal to build a device that helped disabled people to learn better. The prospect of how it could benefit others would be wonderful, but the person's Influencer Self gets involved and makes it about how they will be viewed, how this may impact them, and how they could end up a failure if the idea does not succeed. Such thinking could stop them from staying focused on all the good possibilities the project could provide, which their authentic self knows about.

How to Break Free from Fear

Whenever we are at a point in our lives when we are stuck, we need to identify what fear is at work and where it came from. Once we know this, we can decide how best to navigate this fear.

Most of the time, the things we fear are down to feeling insecure about our inexperience. But inexperience can be worked through by obtaining what we need through extra learning and practice; the rest is down to false associations we hold.

How to make changes:

- **New situations** To address fears arising from totally new situations, ask yourself what you can apply to your man-made fears to provide your brain with the repeated action of having to learn something and store it. What can I learn to better support myself in this new experience?
- **Change your perspective** One way to address fear is to change whom you identify as, what you believe, and what your values are so that you change how you view things or how you are doing things. Ask yourself, Do I need to change my perspective? Am I looking at this in a way that serves me? Are my associations correct?
- **Fearing a situation is happening again** We experience fear when we do not want to get hurt because we perceive a previous situation is happening again. The way to approach this is to

know that we were hurt in the past because our Influencer Self was displaying behaviours it had created. And to realize that just because something went wrong before does not mean it will happen again.

A great philosopher once said, 'Wisdom comes through the understanding of suffering.' As humans, we convince ourselves to believe that if we don't give things much thought, they will go 'wrong'. So we overthink, which creates fearful thoughts. Everything has its time and place on this earth. There is no such thing as things going wrong—learning and wisdom can be obtained in every experience, and every situation has its purpose. There really is nothing to fear because wisdom is riches that money can't buy. And for many of us, we obtain the most wisdom when things go wrong.

Chapter 15
Offenders of Hurt and When We Offend

One of the most practised conditioned behaviours is judgement. Human beings absolutely love to judge others. Without realising it, we pass judgement pretty much all day, every day. We also like to describe ourselves as people who do not judge. Instead, we like to believe we are open and accepting. Yet we all judge—whether we like to accept this or not. When we encounter strangers in public, we look at them up and down and start judging every small detail about them. It is said that we form a first impression about somebody within seven seconds of meeting them.

Finger-Pointing

If we are constantly in a state of judgement, then we are also always in a state of constant deflection. We are very good at pointing out what is amiss with others, deciding what they are doing wrong, comparing ourselves to people, and thinking we would never do the same.

More than judging, what we do even more is point out all the pain and hurt others have caused us. But what does it mean to get hurt? Most of the time, we are left feeling 'hurt' by experiences because they may not have gone according to how we expected them to go.

There is no doubt that sometimes, after having been on the receiving end of being hurt, you have expressed that you would never do what someone did to you. Suppose, for instance, you made an agreement with someone, and while you kept your promises, they didn't keep theirs. You may have said at the time, 'I would never do what they did!' Yet, at another point in your life, you probably did or will do so.

We have the potential to offer acts of love, kindness, giving, and gentleness to the people we care deeply about, but we can also be hurtful, unforgiving, angry, and vengeful. We share experiences with others, get hurt, and perceive *them* as bad, especially if they didn't keep to their end of the bargain. *They* are our offenders of hurt! Rarely do we acknowledge that *we,* too, can be the offender, causing hurt, or that we are never innocent in a situation.

When Relationships End

We will meet many people throughout our lives, forming connections with some of them. Many will have a significant part to play in our growth, but we will also have a part to play in theirs. When we form relationships with people, there are always two sides to it, like two sides of a coin. Some experiences that we form with others will give us happiness, and others will give us some pain—but they are there for their purpose.

If someone you were dating decided they no longer wanted to continue in the relationship they shared with you, but you didn't want it to end, your mind instantly associates it as a betrayal. The hurt stems from your mind searching for all the times when the person promised you they would stay with you forever. You think about all the plans that the two of you had discussed. You imagine being alone and start to panic, thinking about finances, children, and what others will say. Your expectations of the situation have now changed when you didn't want them to, so you are not mentally ready for the change.

Initially, going through hurtful situations like a romantic breakup is not always easy because of all the associations your mind made during the relationship. You now have to try and figure out what is going on, what the next steps are and how you will navigate your new reality—these are scary thoughts.

People Are Allowed to Change Their Minds

People are going to change their minds from time to time. It happens. Are we not allowed to change our minds without it being viewed as a betrayal?

Have you ever changed your mind about something in your life? Haven't you purchased something you loved so much in the store and desperately wanted, only to realize it was all wrong for you once you got home? This is not to say that it is OK to swap your partners for younger versions whenever you feel the need for something new. The point is that what we may want and need today might not be something we want and need further down the line.

The person who ended the relationship may have recognised that the relationship wasn't healthy anymore. They might have seen the truth long before you did. It does hurt when people make decisions about relationships involving you, especially if you are not ready to understand. At times, it may be that the other person has grown in different directions or what they want has changed. Then they'd be the first to recognise the relationship has to end even though they knew the decision would be difficult. Coming to understand what you learned from the experience will likely only happen after it's over.

When we are hurt because a person makes a decision to end things, we need to understand there was no deliberate desire to betray or cause hurt. It is just our perception that is seeing this in the other person. We also have had to make difficult choices that might have caused others pain from time to time.

One day, it may be you who needs to go back on your word. Not only will it be necessary for your growth, but it will probably also be necessary for the other person's growth—but if they are in pain, it may be a while before they see and accept it.

People may enter our lives for us both to learn something about ourselves. And it may be for this reason only and nothing else that their experience with us is meant to be short, even though we perhaps believed that the relationship was going to last forever.

Change Comes from Evolving

Your choices come from your Evolved Mental Maturity. And because it keeps evolving, some relationships can't go on. The person you have shared experiences with may have been running race two with you, but both of you are unable to finish the race together for whatever reason. One of you may make decisions and take certain actions so they don't finish that race with you. Their choices move them onto their third race and leave you on race number two.

You will go on and eventually run your third race too. But you can't do that because there are things that you need to learn about yourself that you were unable to while running the race with that person. Also, remember that there have been times—and will be in the future—when it is you who needs to end things before someone else wants to. Then it is you breaking your promises and causing pain.

Here is a question to think about. Look back on past relationships and when you finally got yourself to a place where you could learn from hurtful experiences and move on to something much better. Now ask, Was your offender 'wrong' for making the decisions they did?

Karma

When we are on the receiving end of being hurt, we must not seek vengeance or constantly point fingers and judge who caused us pain. We view those who cause us hurt as our 'offenders', as though they did something *to* us as opposed to potential growth for you both. When we blame our offenders for causing us hurt, either we want to hurt them back or tend to speak of karma. People often say they hope their offenders will get their karma—yet this is just another form of seeking vengeance.

Most of us misinterpret what karma actually is. We use and associate hurt, blame, and vengeance with karma. When we feel someone has mistreated us, we say things like, 'We hope they get their karma.' Karma does not go after people who are making choices for growth, even if it has caused someone 'hurt.' The perception of hurt depends on our conditioning.

We are all witnesses to people living on the street. There is no denying that many appear to have an addiction. Initially, most of them may not become homeless because of their addiction. They are people just like us who have gone through hurtful, painful, and upsetting experiences that they believe were caused by others. Unfortunately, they have been unable to carry on and climb their fourth hill. Instead, they found a spot in the desert to stop and, eventually, this led them to living on the street. Homeless people tell their stories and experiences in the same way we do, talking about how others have caused them hurt and pain. Their stories are about how people have offended them greatly.

Do you think the offenders of the homeless have any idea that the experiences they shared with them contributed to the homeless being on the street or becoming an addict? No, probably not. The offenders are too busy focusing on their own hurt caused by their own offenders.

You can overcome focusing on your offenders by accepting your part in any situation, even if you feel you were the one on the receiving end of pain. Try your hardest to treat any hurtful experience with love, kindness, forgiveness and grace, even when you don't understand it completely. Do this because, in situations where you are the offender, this is what you want others to offer you—love, kindness, forgiveness, and grace. It is how your karma is returned.

The Big Picture

No matter how bad you may feel your offenders were, leave it to the universe to sort out the bigger picture. Don't think about getting even or take vengeful actions, even as hard as it may seem. Offering love and compassion to your worst enemy might seem like the craziest thing to do, but doing something against your Influencer will only add love and compassion to your own life.

If you continue to judge and cause pain back at others through vengeful thoughts and actions, you only become stuck in your journey. So, who are you really hurting? You can't change someone else's conditioned ways. This is out of your control. What you can control is how you contribute to situations.

The real test, the real decision that truly matters on your path, as mentioned, is not how you treat others when they are good to you; it's how you treat them when you feel hurt and betrayed by them.

This is why if you find yourself very confused about a relationship ending because you don't understand the reason just yet, be patient and know that everything will be OK. You are perceiving the hurt through the part of your brain that has learnt to associate things with a false reality. In time, through evolving and learning, you will be able to understand the reasons more. Always trust that there is good in everything. Always trust that there is a hill that is hiding the stream and fruit trees.

There is always a bigger picture. We just can't see it because we are not meant to. If we could see it, how are we meant to learn? Your offender may have only caused you to be hurt because you were viewing it from your second race. We should always offer forgiveness to those who 'change their minds' or 'betray' us. We will all be offenders at one point or another, and rarely will we even know when we are 'offending'.

At some point in your life, you have been hurt, and you have hurt. You have been judged, and you have judged. You have spoken about others and they of you. No one is innocent. Think of those who have caused you hurt, and ask yourself if you would want them to offer you understanding and forgiveness when they see you as having betrayed them.

Chapter 16
Can You Ever Experience True Love?

Love is a word associated with such strong emotion. At some point in your life, you may have thought that you encountered being in love. You may say you know what love is, but after your next experience with someone, which you again thought was love, you admit it wasn't love after all.

So, what is the true meaning of love? We say we want to experience love and be loved, but do we actually know what love is? Most people understand love to be: 'I love you, but only if you give me love too.' Some say love is when you accept people for who they are, yet so many of us still try to change people all the time. Others think that to truly understand what love is, you need to have experienced the pain of loss.

There is another level of love that we have not yet experienced. For us to feel even a glimpse of what true love is, we need to align with our Authentic Selves, and for this, we need to break away from the part of our minds that believes it is there to help us.

When Is It Love?

There are many different types of love that we get to share and experience. There is the love you have for a family member, a child, a partner, a pet, and self-love. The list is continuous. Do we consider all these different types of love to be the same, or are they different? Is there a difference between liking someone and loving them? And, at what point do you transition from liking someone to loving them?

Does it start to become love when you become vulnerable and scared? At what stage does it turn into unconditional love? We have heard about unconditional love, but do humans ever truly experience and give unconditional love when we have so many demands and expectations?

We love someone when they look, act, and treat us in a certain way, and we expect them to behave in ways we would like them to. When we first meet people whom we go on to have intimate relationships with, we fall in love with them. Later during the relationship, we try to change them because they don't meet our further expectations.

Love of Self

When asked if you unconditionally love yourself, most of you would think, 'Of course, I do'. We all have our own perception of reality, so you will love yourself according to where your Evolved Mental Maturity is.

It's doubtful that many of you sit and take the time to give thanks to yourself, shower yourself with gratitude, tell yourself each day about how special you are, and show appreciation to yourself for continuing to show up and be you in everyday life, even when things get tough.

We need to make praising and accepting ourselves a normal practise. Some people do practise this in their lives and do understand its importance, but they are often ridiculed by those around them. When someone talks about themselves positively, it often turns out that others will judge them negatively for it. They are often seen as being conceited and vain, too full of themselves, and as 'their heads can't fit through the door.' We have come to believe that we can't speak highly of ourselves because it means our egos are too big.

Connecting Negatively

So, it isn't easy for us to speak kind words to ourselves and, by extension, to those we know because it's not something we practise consistently. Unfortunately, if we pay close attention, we will see that many human beings connect in a negative way.

What does this mean? Notice how we form relationships. First, we become acquainted with someone. Acquaintances could be anyone we encounter daily, weekly, or monthly, with our main interactions being making small talk when we cross paths. The problem is that small talk is usually on a negative footing.

For example, you may work in an office where people, including a regular delivery man, come and go throughout the day. Every time they come to the office, your conversations with them normally go something like this: 'Gosh, the traffic is bad out there today. Gosh, horrible weather, very wet and gloomy I wouldn't go out there. I am not having a great day. We are so short-staffed, and I am left to do all the work. It's so unfair.' And to be agreeable, you would both respond to each other with the same negativity.

Or suppose you are standing at a bus stop with total strangers. The small talk would consist of complaints. How long you have been waiting for the bus, how the bus is never on time, or how everyone pushes in front of you.

It can be even worse with the people we build friendships with. We moan to each other about our bosses, work colleagues, family members, and everything else. How will we ever be able to move to our next level of consciousness and experience love without expectations if we are all still operating at such a negative vibration?

If we are always connecting negatively, how can we ever be truly accepting of ourselves and others? Many of us do not realise that if our normal practise is to speak negatively of others, we cannot possibly feel positively about ourselves. You may think that you don't talk negatively about yourself, but this is a bit of a false reality.

Your brain is linked to how you perceive things. Your brain does not have some magic divide (as previously mentioned) where it thinks, 'I only associate negative thoughts with others, and I view myself positively.' If it is your view that it is OK to speak badly of others, and you do so regularly, then it is certain that you also speak of yourself in negative ways as well—even though you may think that you have positive regard for yourself. It all stems from the fact that you have learnt to view yourself in a certain way, which you then project onto others.

Learning to Connect Positively

If it were your normal practise to wake up every day thinking and saying sweet, kind, caring, and encouraging things to yourself, eventually, it could come naturally to you to say the same things about others. Your conversation would go something like this: 'Hi, how great is it that we got to have some rain today? What a wonderful day it is. I am feeling great today. I am really proud of myself today for having pushed through some challenging situations. How about you? What great things are you doing later?'

How do we connect more positively? If we were to look at people who are liked and respected by people, they often do not go searching for it. They naturally attract respect because they respect themselves and others, and they show this in how they speak and act—they live and breathe it. Many people who demand respect don't get it because they do not respect themselves or anyone else, yet expect others to automatically respect them because they think they are entitled to it.

If you want to be treated with genuine love and kindness, you will receive it if it is who you are internally and what you put out into the world already. If you were renowned for always moaning about every hardship in life, people who encountered you would pick that up and join you in conversations about hardships and dislikes. Human beings often find common goals with people to get along with them. What you feel within is what you will give off, whether you know it or not.

We Receive Who We Are

Whatever you give off into the world is returned to you because it is how you perceive things to be. The universe might send you an amazing opportunity that could help change your life for the better, but if your mindset is always negative, you will never be able to see it for what it is. It could be a wonderful opportunity, one with the potential to manifest in magical ways, yet if you only view what can go wrong, you'll never be able to act on it. Your negative mindset has stood in your way.

This is why, to find and experience the loving relationships we wish for, we first need to find that loving relationship with ourselves. We will never find the positivity and love 'out there' somewhere if we are not ready. This is because we still have work to be done on ourselves and our mindset. Once you take the steps to change internally, you can change things externally.

Some people have a big misconception that if they are good to others, they will appear weak and be taken advantage of. Thinking this way has the potential to stop you from moving forward—being kind, loving, and forgiving will never go against you. You may come across people stuck in their Evolved Mental Maturity, so they have adapted to dealing with life by just taking from others. If you come across people like this, know your boundaries and be clear when deciding how much to give.

We need to change the way we have learnt to connect. Once we align with our true, positive, uplifting self-identifying labels, we will be able to connect to others with love. Once we show ourselves love, then we can offer love without conditions. And loving without conditions is how we experience the essence of what true love is.

Chapter 17
Substitutions and Habits

Sometimes, we have experiences that make us feel like we just can't keep our self-worth and belief on an even keel. We may have had one too many disappointments or knockbacks in life, so we haven't been able to shake ourselves out of a negative head space. We may feel lost, trapped, or stuck, like our emotions are totally out of control or we are drowning.

At these times, it is easy to fall prey to our Influencers, such as believing we have no choices. Our Influencers make things seem much bigger or scarier than they actually are. This is when we so often experience symptoms of stress, anxiety, anger, loneliness, resentment, depression, and so on.

When life hands us experiences that we allow to affect our self-worth and belief, and we don't have the support or life direction to figure things out, many of us tend to use substitutions to help us cope.

How Substitutions Work

We all have, at some point while experiencing difficult times, tried using an external substance, thing or activity to relieve some of the feelings we can't get a handle on. These activities are called substitutions because we are substituting the substance or activity for the real problem.

Common substitutions are food, drugs, gambling, sex, shopping, or anything else that provides a 'high' or short-lived release (that takes someone out of themselves). They all appear to provide some sort of escape from the problems someone is facing. However, over time, any substitution turns into a coping mechanism, then becomes a habit, and finally, can lead to a serious addiction. In this way, what just appears to be a harmless substitution can have a detrimental effect. And the original reason why someone started using substitutions becomes lost, buried deep within them while the habit of addiction takes hold.

Our bodies are pretty incredible, they fight against illness and mend themselves to function in an orderly manner, yet we certainly take for granted how great they are. Unfortunately, instead of loving and respecting our bodies, we damage them with the behavioural habits we create by using substitutions.

Our brains learn and then store information in our subconscious for later when we need to rely on it. As was previously discussed, we can't tap into the brain to pinpoint exactly how we have learnt something. Take, for example, walking. We know how to walk, and we do it without any conscious thought process. We all know that we had to learn how to walk. And even though we don't remember how we did it, our subconscious does. It's a memory that is stored in our brains.

Why Habits Are Difficult to Change

The same applies to all of your habits. You don't know where they came from, and you don't know exactly how they started. However, your brain easily allows your habits to kick in time and time again. As the old saying goes, 'Humans are creatures of habit.'

This is why we find it so hard to change habits straight away. Our brains cannot tell us exactly how and when our habits began. Perhaps it is just something we were never meant to know or are yet to discover. Most habits are linked to emotions originating in some life experience and stored in our subconscious.

Food Conditioning

A very common substitute that many people use is food. Using food to help us cope can lead to obesity, bulimia, binging, and anorexia—and these are just the more serious results of using food as a substitute. Behavioural habits that are part of us can stem from very early life experiences. Also, the source of a habit can be a learnt behaviour passed down from many earlier generations.

As a nation, we have always used food as a comfort, which is why human beings are emotional eaters. Using food as a substitute is so naturally accepted in society that it isn't seen as a massive problem. At some point in your life, going back to when you were a child, situations occurred where your brain learnt to use food as a source of comfort. Without realising it, you use the same habit of substitution as an adult. Furthermore, you have probably given little thought to how your eating habits developed, and if you did think about it, you'd have no idea where they stemmed from.

It can only be surmised that there were many situations in your life where, as a young child, your brain very innocently formed an association of comfort to food or certain foods. Here is one illustration. As a toddler, you tripped and scraped your knee when playing out in the garden. Right away, you started to cry because of your surprise and your knee hurting. The actual pain didn't last very long; however, your mum came over, checked to see if you were OK and then gave you ice cream as she said, 'Here, have this ice cream. It will make you feel better.' You start to eat the ice cream and instantly feel happier. Even though it may have been your mother's caring for you or the fact that the pain lasted only moments that really cheered you up, feeling better was associated in your brain with ice cream.

There could have been other incidents where your parents soothed you with food, saying, 'Have these sweets. They will make it all better.' When you were tired, they may have given you a bottle to settle you when, in fact, you didn't need it. These well-meaning gestures probably continued for the remainder of your childhood. And each one reinforced in your brain that unsettled emotions are relieved with food.

So, this process that taught you to associate food with settling emotions is called non-direct conditioned teaching. But it constructed a false reality. It was not the actual ice cream that took away the pain and made you feel better. Your pain from any unpleasant incidents was over in a split second. You were absolutely fine and would have settled and moved on with or without the food. But it was the *suggested belief* by the adult that the ice cream would ease the pain that led to your conditioning. It is like the placebo effect.

Eating for the Mind, not the Body

Unfortunately, in conditioned learning, your brain stores the information in your subconscious mind, so you have no idea how such a simple thing as turning to ice cream every time you are upset began. It was handed to you with the suggestion that it makes things better.

It must also be noted that the prior generations and our society didn't just teach us to use food to cope with negative emotions. We eat for our happy emotions as well, like celebrations and get-togethers. Conditioned behaviours are such mindless acts that they truly don't serve us to the point where their influence on us can be detrimental.

So because of all this, we tend to eat for our minds and not for our actual bodies. And this is why you can lose all the weight you need to lose through healthy or even fad diets because you set yourself a short-lived goal and stuck to it. But after that fad diet has finished, if you do not address the underlying cause of what you are going through (like recognising every time you are substituting food for your emotions), in no time, you'll be back to packing on all the weight you lost. It only takes having a bad day at work or a fallout with someone to trigger that emotional eating, so you find yourself reaching for food again to help you cope and ease how you feel.

The positive effects of feeding our bodies nutritious foods are very clear. Healthy food benefits our bodies and minds, while junk food does absolutely nothing but make us feel worse. Yet we unconsciously torture our bodies with the habits we have created to help us cope with our emotions. All because we have not come to understand where all our behaviours came from and because some of our behaviours are so naturally accepted.

Replacement

Initially, what seems like a harmless one-off incident, repeated, results in creating deeper patterns and habits. Then our existence becomes about living in these cycles that we keep repeating. Thoughts—emotions—fix—happy—guilt—regret. Then you get to the point where you can't imagine life without your substitutions and rely on them, thus destroying your life through addictions and compulsive behaviours. We can't reach and progress to high-achieving levels when we remain stuck in these vicious cycles, often without even realising or understanding that we are doing it.

Sometimes when we kick one habit, all that happens is we replace one substitution with another. This happens because there are still emotions, past upsets, or even new ones that have not been dealt with completely. Replacement happens because we still need a coping mechanism, which can get you into even more hot water.

For example, someone realizes they smoke cigarettes to help with emotions of stress and anger. They are proud when they finally give up smoking but seem unaware that they've started drinking more, in particular after situations that bring up these same emotions. They then become more dependent on alcohol to help them cope. Only when they learn to identify correctly and respond to their learnt behaviours will they break the pattern and not rely on any more substitutions.

Choice

We each have a choice in every situation, and options are presented to us every second of the day. We already have so much to figure out in living every day—discovering our lessons, evolving through each stage of life, understanding our conditioning, habits, and patterns and learning how to align with our Authentic Self. It's a burden and complication to add in coping with compulsive behaviours around substitutions like drugs, food, gambling or shopping. We need to choose to stay away from the things that have been proven to be bad for us because we already have so much to sort out.

There are ways to release the unsettling emotions you feel. Your reactions are your actions. You can continue to choose an action that will provide a quick fix, but it will also provide more negative feelings that will contribute to damaging your self-worth. Or you can choose an action that releases natural, feel-good endorphins that can also instantly shift your feelings. These positive, more natural substitutions include exercising, talking about your feelings, or engaging in creative outlets.

But, with anything in life, everything has the potential to be good or bad. Man can abuse even what is good. Take drugs, for instance, which can be life-changing and life-saving. Yet human beings can also abuse drugs to the point of death. So, even if it is generally agreed that exercise and healthy eating can greatly help people by contributing to a balanced and positive mindset, even these activities can potentially lead to problems. With a negative head space, someone could become obsessive about healthy eating and exercising compulsively. Any negative feelings about their body or low self-esteem may potentially drive someone to extremes, causing them to over-train and not eat very much and creating further problems and destructive patterns.

All the substitutions you use in life today began with one incident when your mind believed that it had been given a release from a situation. It didn't recognize there was no real release because once the substitution wore off, the underlying issue or feeling would still be there.

Working with Your Influencer

We all have impulses, urges, underlying feelings and discomforts within our subconscious. So how do we make the necessary changes?

If you become the Observer in your life and Self-Reflect, you start to recognise and observe behavioural patterns and when you are acting out of habit. It is possible to stop yourself and release some of these patterns. Breaking habits takes persistent effort. You won't get it right all the time, especially since we can't always:

1. See or know what triggered engaging in an old habit, or

2. Pinpoint how and when the actual habit pattern began.

But now that you understand that your patterns and habits, at times, were formed because of conditioned learning, this will help you to better stay aligned rather than react with old habits. When dealing with any experience, no one knows you better than you know yourself. Identify when your Influencer Self is bringing out the mental and behavioural patterns it has learnt, then work alongside your Observer and Responsive to stay out of the old methods of being in the world.

Anyone who is a confident driver understands that someone can't get into a car on the first attempt and begin to drive. Learning to drive, like so much else, is a process. Working with your Influencer is a process too. Changing your habits will all be part of a process.

Chapter 18
Comfort Zones

What is Your Comfort Zone?

The previous chapter explained how we use substitutions to help us cope when we experience feelings of discomfort. This behaviour forms part of what is described as your comfort zone, which you have probably heard people talk about. These phrases are probably familiar to you: 'You will never change your life until you step out of your comfort zone' and 'Change begins at the end of your comfort zone.'

Your comfort zone plays a vital part in deciding whether you will achieve things or remain stagnant in your life. Your conditioned and learnt behavioural patterns are all part of your comfort zone, such as when your mind has made certain associations, like believing that a particular substitution helps you cope. There are areas within your comfort zone. One area has to do with what associations your brain has formed about every one of your emotions.

Certainty

Another area in your comfort zone is where your brain has associated feelings of safety with certainty. Your

Influencer-Self loves to convince you that situations do not feel safe if there is no certainty about them. Because most outcomes are unknown, we are hesitant to make decisions, move forward or try to achieve our goals and desires, especially regarding things that might not have gone well for us in the past.

In areas where we have experienced hurt, disappointment and loss, we find ourselves afraid to try again because we don't want to be 'hurt' yet another time. Your thoughts tell you to run away from new situations or enter them only partially to avoid going through the same experience and emotions. Your brain may even unknowingly sabotage a situation because of not wanting to go through emotions of pain and hurt.

But the irony of comfort zones is that, even if you avoid what you fear, you are still left with feelings of emptiness and longing for what you haven't done because your brain told you it was too scary. Your thoughts will say: 'I really want that thing, and I'm not getting it. Why can't I have what everyone else has?' It's a catch-22. Either way, you won't feel good.

When confronted with something new, there will be natural nervousness as it is something the brain has not learnt about before, but it doesn't last for very long. For instance, when someone starts at a new school, they feel nervous and scared on the first day. Yet, by the time they finish that first day, those initial feelings of nervousness are gone, and they are excited to return to school the next day.

There are no clear paths and no guarantees in life. There isn't even a guarantee that we will wake up tomorrow morning. Part of the process of life is not only to experience what is familiar to us but also to engage in what is new or feels foreign. We learn more through confronting what is unknown than known. If we are too complacent, we often only see life through one lens.

Control

Another well-known and common technique that we use to feel safe and in our comfort zones is desiring or asserting control. The need for control also ties in with wanting certainty about the unknown. We believe that if we can control situations, there is less chance that things will go wrong. But we don't realise that being in control never allows us to fully explore situations for what they can be. Being in control is one way of never stepping into uncertainty. We believe we can safeguard ourselves from our failings, but control masks a greater insecurity in us.

For example, suppose someone has met a potential partner and started a relationship with them, but their biggest insecurity is that they will be cheated on again based on past experiences. An overriding feeling of fear that the new partner will cheat pushes the person to act out and become controlling. The fear is triggered when the partner says they are going out, and the person starts thinking, 'What if they cheat on me when they go out? What if they meet someone at work?' So, the person starts to demand that the partner can't go out or suggests that they go along with the partner everywhere they go, pretending they want to spend time with them. This offers their mind reassurance and comfort that the possibility of cheating is controlled if the partner doesn't go out at all or only goes out with the person.

In a scenario like this one, you try to control everything in the relationship because control provides you with a false sense of security. It allows you to remain living in your comfort zone. Yet you are also continuously living through your Influencer. You choose to run away from what needs addressing. Eventually, one way or another, you will create the scenario of cheating or push the relationship apart because of your control issues.

We Will Always Have to Self-Reflect

No matter how evolved we are—how much we think we know or think we are getting right or have learnt and changed—we will continue to act and behave in ways that cause us to always have to **Self-Reflect** about our behaviours and actions. This is, in part, because we will always snap right back into our conditioning and our comfort zones.

I wrote this book years ago in 2015, sent it off to an editor, and self-published it. A few copies were printed, and I left them in a drawer. Yet the thought of what I wanted to achieve never left me, though I did nothing about it. I picked up the book again in 2021 and reread it. The essence of my thinking was still in there, but I felt I had personally moved into a new understanding and wanted to change some of it. Well, that didn't happen. I pretty much rewrote the entire book. I found the whole revision process to be tremendously difficult. Despite having already written the book, I still found revising it to be tiresome. There was an inner battle within me about whether I should dedicate the time and effort to complete it. I faced major internal resistance, yet I knew deep down that this was it. This time, I would take it forward and follow through wholeheartedly. It meant I would just have to face the uncertainty of starting from the beginning again. This was going against my comfort zone because I already had a career in another industry I'd spent twenty years doing.

This book is who I am. But it is also the part of me that hardly anyone gets to see.

Luckily, I am not prone to questions constantly circulating in my head like, 'What if it doesn't work? What if no one understands what I am trying to share? What if I did all this for nothing? What if I fail? I don't have these types of conscious thoughts because I don't view life this way. I understand some of how my brain works—about behavioural patterns and habits and everything else written in this book.

But what I was doing, or my resistance was doing, was every time I went to my computer and started to write, after ten minutes, I would search for a spelling of a word. Then after I had done that, I would search for the weather forecast. And I would maybe buy some dog food or look at houses that were up for sale. Then at times, I would think I was hungry, so I would look for food or that I had had a long day and was tired, so I needed to sleep as I didn't want to burn myself out and feel tired at work the next day.

Pushing Forward

While this was happening, I knew perfectly well what I was doing. I knew it because by being the Observer, I knew I was killing time, procrastinating, and not giving it the real effort I knew I could. Meanwhile, I knew deep down that it didn't matter if people didn't get what I write about as long as I did. This was where my inner battles were—stalling and knowing others would also see this part of me.

In fact, you are reading this because I did push forward. But those deep-rooted behavioural patterns of fearing something totally new and uncertain to me tried, from time to time, to creep up and push me back into my comfort zone and keep my Influencer Self in charge. This is why, at times, you may feel like you have taken a step forward, thinking you are doing well, only to find you have taken two steps back.

Consider the example of someone choosing to go on a diet for three months. They lose six pounds, feel great about all their hard work, and most ironically, they then say, 'I am going to reward myself with a takeaway!' Choosing to have a takeaway as a reward is not helping you move away from your pattern. It only keeps you in it because your brain still associates unhealthy food with something positive. But the greasy meal is not positive in the slightest. Viewing the takeaway in this way is partly how your brain got you into trouble in the first place. Changing the part of your brain that has associated food with reward is not to view the takeaway as a reward.

If you ask anyone nearing the end of their life, 'What is the one thing you would go back and change'? They will all tell you they regret the things they didn't do. Nobody regrets what they've done, but they do regret what they didn't do—the things that linger in their minds because they were too worried about the unknown. Time is something we will never get back. Are you going to keep allowing yourself to only live in your comfort zone?

Chapter 19
Time and the Quick-Fix Mindset

Our brains have a very unusual perception of time. The things we crave and so desperately want in life seem to take a very long time, yet when we want situations to end, it seems to take forever for them to be over. People count down the days they have to work until they can be off, sometimes feeling like it drags on forever. Then the opposite occurs when it comes to the days off. They can feel like time flies by, and it wasn't much time off at all.

Another strange way time is perceived is how, when we were young teenagers, most of us could not wait to grow up and be adults, and it felt like it would never happen. Now that we are adults, we wish we had stayed young longer and reminisce about the 'good old days.'

Why do humans perceive time in such skewed ways? Where did the human concept of time even originate? Just like our habits and patterns originated from our conditioning, how we view time is also part of our conditioned learning through the generations. Furthermore, how we approach time is not only due to our conditioned behaviour but today is also influenced by the evolution of technology. In addition, as in the example above, I believe that our feelings and experiences towards a situation also create and determine our perception of what time is.

How Energy Affects How We View Time

Negative emotions are normally associated with feeling heavy, drained and exhausted. In contrast, positive emotions can be identified as feeling light with childlike freedom and joy. Suppose someone went through the very negative experience of being bullied at school. Those school days felt to them like they were never going to end. They were petrified, anxious and scared so much that they dreaded school days and felt the holidays couldn't come quickly enough.

Then, the opposite occurs when someone is having a positive experience. Suppose someone has gone on holiday somewhere sunny and relaxing for two weeks. During the holiday, they felt relaxed, stress-free and extremely happy to be there. The lightness of their feelings during the holiday made them feel like it was flying by. As the end of the holiday came closer, they wished they could stay a bit longer and actually started to dread when it would be over. They start to think that soon they will have to return to reality! They begin to panic about going back to work and continuing to live such a stressful life.

If you felt the same feelings in your 'reality' as you did on holiday, the holiday wouldn't feel too short because all the same feelings would just continue upon your return. But because you view and associate your 'real world' with stress, your concept of time differs then. So, your brain develops its own perception of time because of its association with the thoughts and feelings generated during different experiences.

Technology and Instant Results

Technology has evolved immensely; because of this, our perception of time has further changed over the years. We are living in a world where everything moves at a much quicker pace. Yet, just decades ago, before computers, people communicated through letters. Before trains, cars and air travel, it was normal for people to send messages to each other through someone on foot or horse or by boat. If we were to compare this to how we communicate today, we would perceive that way of communicating to be ever so slow.

We are now in an advanced technological era, so we naturally live in a faster-paced environment. Because of this, we are looking for instant solutions—our concept of time has moved on to a quick-fix mindset. If something takes too long to do, it is viewed as 'too much hard work'.

With technology, so much is instant—at the click of a button. Because of this, our perception of time makes us think things can happen overnight. We want instant success, instant weight loss, and instant money. And we believe all we have to do to obtain it is to marry a footballer, be a footballer, become instantly rich and famous by being an influencer or gamer on social media, bet on the stock market, or win a fortune by buying scratch cards. We want to cut as many corners as possible, while we don't want to do anything that requires some long-term effort for lasting results. And we love to use excuses for not doing something by claiming we don't have the time.

We are impatient and don't want to wait around. We want changes to happen straight away. An Internet site takes too long to load, which in reality is taking seconds. We become so impatient waiting for it; how on earth will we make changes that require effort and consistency for longer than a minute?

Effort

Effort is an action that does not appeal to someone if they have a quick-fix mentality, which most of us now have. In fact, our minds are conditioned to see putting in effort as something negative—it is often associated with extra tiresome activities. Who wants to make an effort when we can get something without any effort instantly?

Imagine telling an adolescent in today's society that if they wanted to communicate with someone who lived far away, they would need to travel on four trains and four buses to reach the person and would have to repeat this every time they needed to communicate with them. They would look at you as if you were mad. Sending a text message via phone is so accessible, quick, and requires little exertion, but even sending a text message nowadays can seem like an effort, so we send voice notes instead.

To achieve anything, whether a goal, a relationship, an education, or a career path, we need to change how our brain perceives effort because there is no achievement without it.

Effort is focused energy. And as previously discussed, where you put your focus is what you will attract into your life. However, just focusing on something is not enough; part of that focus must include effort. Climbing out of bed in the morning requires effort, as does taking a shower and commuting to work. Effort is energy; energy is effort. Even making a choice requires some sort of effort. It might not be a physical effort, but it is a mental one.

We often view people who have achieved as luckier or having had an easier life than us. Our brains are trying to protect us again by making us feel good about ourselves. Yet it is just providing us with falsehoods about others in order to give us excuses to stay settled in our comfort zones.

Everything in life is a process. Humans have measured these processes with time, and because we have done this, we consider some processes as taking too long or requiring too much effort. Part of every single process in life is putting in effort without being able to see the end results.

Consider, for example, when people struggle to lose weight. Many tend to give up after the first week or even the first few days because the weight takes far too long to come off so the results are not instant. There is no quick fix to dieting. Like many others in life, weight loss is one of those things where you have to put in the effort without experiencing instant results. A lot of the effort that is required comes from your belief, trust, perseverance, and understanding that results will manifest by the end of your process. Sound like too much effort?

The irony about how we have come to dislike effort is that, without realising it, we put in effort every day of our lives without seeing immediate results. We do this when we are waiting for our salaries. Every morning we go to work, even when we feel tired, depressed, anxious, bored, or fed up. We continue to do this every day. We don't physically see any money, but we know we will be paid by the end of the month. If we don't go to work, we won't get paid. And if we don't get paid, we can't pay the bills. In other words, we all are capable of applying effort to the things we want, even when it takes some time.

Talking Yourself Out of It

A sad consequence of having a quick-fix mindset is that we convince ourselves not to go for a particular goal or dream if it would take too long. Similarly, we talk ourselves out of going for our dreams if the path to get there is unconventional.

An example is when someone is at a stage in life where they want to change careers, and part of the process would require them to spend four years going back to college or university. After that, they'd start over from the bottom and work their way up.

Suppose this was you. You have the money to do this, and it sounds simple enough, but you are turning fifty. When you think about it, your brain starts to focus on your age and tells you that you are 'too old'. Doing the math, it calculates that you will be about 58 or 60 years old before you actually have enough experience in your new field to be taken seriously.

Most people are often put off by the whole idea of what goes into a career change and don't pursue what they so desperately want. Instead, they choose to stay in their existing careers and remain unhappy because of their comfort zone's false reality that it keeps them safe. But there is so much irony in thinking this way because the time will pass anyway. Staying where they are won't slow down becoming 58. Whether they spend the next four years in education or not, the time still passes. Do not allow your concept of time or the fear of effort to keep you from doing what you want.

There is No End to Processing

Regarding a quick-fix mindset, another thing that you need to keep in the forefront of your mind is that with every process, there is no end to the process. The word 'end' relates to being final; however, few processes in life are ever finished. Once you achieve something, you don't say, 'OK, that is enough now. I know everything. Nothing else is required.'

Effort is continuous. Our whole life is a continuous process that constantly requires effort. Let your next effort be learning how to recognise when your comfort zone wants you to fall back into complacency and the habits and patterns that made you stop wanting to achieve or put in effort.

There are fundamental laws in life that cannot be changed, like what goes up must come down, before day must come night, and before summer must come spring. But there is another fundamental law in life: **Consistent effort only occurs through your belief and trust in what might be. You must trust life and trust your process.**

Chapter 20
Understanding Energy

Our energy is just as important as the oxygen we breathe. Everything we do requires energy. We cannot see or touch it, yet it is crucial to our existence.

The energy within and around our bodies is like the electricity running through an electrical cable. We can't see the electricity going through the cable, but we know it's there. Sometimes it is difficult for us to understand our energy because it doesn't take a physical form for our brains to comprehend fully—yet our energy is part of who we are. And it is part of who others are.

Sometimes when we enter a room, for example, we can pick up that something is not right because the people there have just had an argument. There is a heaviness to the space and the people. Also, we can meet people for the first time and get a funny feeling about them; something doesn't feel right. It's their energy we're feeling. Equally, we can meet someone else who gives off a good feeling.

But what is this energy of ours? We often hear people speak about energy, we can pick up these feelings relating to energy, but we can't see it. Energy is who we all are beyond our physical form. It's within and around us and makes up everything we are—our physical body, personality, brain, presence, workings, and our Authentic Self.

One of our most important choices in life is how we choose to manage our energy.

The Energy Put in Determines the Time Healing Takes

Many of us have formed romantic relationships with people. In some of these experiences, we may have endured pain and discomfort when they ended. Our friends and family offered us support and used encouraging words like, 'You will get through this. Time is a healer. Don't worry; in time, you will feel better.' And over time, things did get better—the pain subsided, we became less consumed with constant thoughts about the situation, and, eventually, we got to a point where we felt that we had moved on. Most people believe it was 'time' that made the pain easier, and this is partly true. Time does have a part to play in any healing process.

But why is it that some hurtful experiences feel like it takes forever to forget them and move on, and others seem to take no time at all? Just as was discussed in the previous chapter, this perception is about how we view time. We can't know how long it will take to process our feelings or past experience.

However, we can know the approximate amount of time it will take to move past a painful experience because it depends on how much energy we invest in the healing process.

A phone takes a certain amount of time and electrical watts to charge fully. After that, it doesn't gain any extra charge if it is left plugged in. All that is occurring is a waste of energy, which is costing you. In the same way, when someone takes years to get over a hurtful experience, it's like they kept their phone on charge beyond the time and watts it needed to reach a hundred percent.

The length of time someone's process takes is determined by how much energy they invest. If someone in a person's past did something that they felt was unforgivable and left them hurt, the person might remain angry at them and even make it their mission to pay them back. Maybe they would spend time constantly thinking of ways to hurt their offender, like checking out their socials every minute of the day. The offender becomes the primary focus of the person whose thoughts are negative, unforgiving, and spiteful because they are acting out their pain. Soon the person's entire focus and energy, everything they do, is about the offender.

By having these types of thoughts, feelings and actions, the person has allowed themselves to stay connected to their offender and the pain. They may not have any contact at all with the offender, but the connection is still an energetic one. Moreover, in a situation like this, someone is allowing themselves to remain in an overcharge of energy and at risk of remaining stuck in that energy field. All that focus is being wasted when their energy could be used to work on ways to help them move forward instead.

Continuing the analogy, in addition to overcharging ourselves, it is possible to undercharge as well—like when we unplug the phone early before it's charged to one hundred per cent. We do this by forcing ourselves to move on from a hurtful experience too soon. Instead of working through our understanding of the hurt, we bury our thoughts and emotions with substitutions or new experiences, pretending that we are fine and haven't been affected in any way. Both these ways of using our energy are not helpful.

Moving on from an experience becomes easier once we no longer focus on the person or the experience and accept that the relationship was not meant to be. In essence, we are no longer allowing the phone to be charged with that energy and have pulled the plug, so to speak. We have a choice about the amount of 'time' it takes to move on from hurtful experiences—we can use the energy to think and do things that keep us overcharging and wasting our energy, or we can choose to do and think of things to help us realise when to pull the plug once it is at hundred per cent. Everything lies within us.

Vibrating at Different Frequencies

Everyone vibrates at different energy frequencies depending mainly on their level of evolvement. As we go through different stages of life, so will our energy. When we positively evolve, our frequency changes. The reverse happens too. People can become stuck or confused so that negativity enters their fields and remains with them.

If you surround yourself with others who vibrate at lower energy frequencies than you, your energy may get entwined with theirs if you are not careful. Over time, you may align with that frequency and display the same behaviours as those people. People who vibrate at lower energy levels also tend to want to keep you with them at their level. They will try to manipulate you into thinking you are the same as they are and can slowly take your energy away from you, leaving you feeling drained or low until your energy matches theirs.

Victim Energy

John was generally positive. Though he had gone through some hurtful experiences, he had always tried to remain optimistic. He met a woman who appeared at first glance to be happy and kind. Then as time went on, she started to tell John stories about all the things she had been through—how tragic her childhood was, how others always put her down, how everyone at school ganged up on her and how she didn't have any friends because of it. She also struggled to find a job because no one liked her, and others seemed to get all the opportunities except her.

Initially, none of it sounded too alarming. In fact, John understood her childhood stories, felt sorry for her, and wanted to protect and care for her. Soon though, there were other signs of a problem. She always made subtle excuses for why she could not join him in doing things so that John had to pick up all the responsibilities in the relationship. It slowly started to interfere and overlap with John's life. His dreams and goals began to take a back seat, and he didn't socialise with his friends and family anymore. All he seemed to be doing was tending to her needs, as she was unable to do anything for herself.

The woman is an example of someone with victim energy. This type of person will, sooner or later, get us to adapt to their way of thinking and being—and they do this because then we are no threat to their frequency. Victim energy can be very draining and can certainly pull us down. Someone can appear very innocent to begin with, but after a while, we might start to feel trapped. If we're not careful and keep allowing people with victim or other lower energy into our lives, it can eventually take control of us and leave us feeling very powerless.

It is important to allow the correct type of energy into your field. That's not to say we should not enter any personal or professional relationships. We simply need to be mindful that some of the conditioned behaviours and choices of others can cause them to vibrate at lower frequencies, which can slowly penetrate, influence, and erode our energy without us realising it. Through observation, we can be mindful and, when possible, choose not to be around it too much.

Focus Energy Positively

Our choices are also about energy. With every choice, we create a ripple effect in our energy. Our lives operate through so many energetic channels that we cannot see but can only feel. We make choices every minute of the day, and all our choices affect our energy just as much as the people around us do.

If you keep making decisions that do not serve you, you will remain in a whirlwind of energy that keeps you rotating round and round until you eventually become blocked. You will always remain in overcharge, which is costly to your well-being.

Through our choices, we can nurture our energy, safeguard it and ensure that we vibrate at the levels where we want to be. Many energies are positive and good, like that of trees, grass, animals, and the sea and sun. The energy of nature always uplifts and calms us, which is why we feel at peace when surrounded by it. It's our solace, so we should use it to nurture ourselves. This is also true of our connections with people; they can be our solace or a major disruption in our energy fields.

If you focus your energy positively on something and keep at it consistently, you will eventually get the results you want. The more we invest our energy into something, the more it grows. What does bear keeping in mind, as stated before, is that, sometimes, the things we think we want are not necessarily the things we need.

If you have spent all your time focusing your energy on something that didn't go the way you wanted, let go of the disappointment and know that you may still be exhibiting some patterns and behaviours that may need releasing before you are a vibrational match to what you want.

Continue to nurture your energy by making choices that help you vibrate at a higher frequency. Always remember that, like everything we have discussed so far, being clear about where you focus your energy is a process and requires effort. It requires Self-Reflection and observation. But being at the highest vibrational frequency that you can be given your level of Evolved Mental Maturity means that you are in your authentic self.

This concludes Part III. You've come very far now. You've read and understand all the ways your Influencer can work in your life—through your conditioning, self-identifying beliefs, expectations, fear, offenders of hurt, substitutions and comfort zones. You've also learned about relationships, time, and energy. But above all, you've learned that what you get out of life is all up to you. It's your choice. You can choose to process, Self-Reflect, observe, and be grateful or not. The results will depend on your effort. The results depend on you.

In Part IV, the next section, you will learn what Life Purpose is really about and how it connects to living authentically.

Part IV

Your Purpose

Chapter 21
Your Purpose Is to Find Your Authentic Self

Has there ever been a time in your life when you have asked yourself, Why am I here on this earth? What am I destined to do? What is my purpose?

Achieving Is Not Life Purpose

Some people believe that expressing the talents they were born with is what their Life Purpose is all about. So, for example, if someone is gifted with a good voice, their purpose is to be a singer. But is this true? When people achieve what they pursue because they believe it to be their destiny to do so, does it mean they have also found and achieved their life purpose?

Some of us have accomplished certain things in life, like a partner, a car, or a nice house, yet there is still a consistent feeling that there is more to life, and it won't go away, so we just don't feel fulfilled. We may even go so far as believe that those things mean we've achieved some of our Life Purpose but still feel dissatisfied.

Not a Sudden Realization

Others feel they have not yet found their Life Purpose and believe it will eventually become clear. Finding purpose does not mean that someone jumps out of bed one day and says, 'Hey guys, I had a dream last night and now finally know what my purpose is.' Some grand, one-shot situation or near-death experience won't catapult them into finding their purpose.

Most of us still feel unfulfilled in our lives even after many achievements because we are not aligning with our Authentic Selves.

Accomplishments Can Be the Influencer

Our achievements may have come from our Influencers, which can accomplish great things and reap many rewards. Yet all the success still leaves us 'feeling empty'. The Influencer Self is the part of us that has learnt the human way of how to achieve. It believes it must do or have certain things on this earth to be successful.

Through no fault of your own, you may be doing things for all the wrong reasons and because of your Influencer's belief that they are necessary for this life.

The Life Purpose Triangle

So, what does it mean to find your purpose? Our true journey here on earth is to break away from our Influencers. We do this by navigating through our Life Purpose Triangle. With each experience in life, in our day-to-day interactions, through our goals and dreams, we may be living in ways that do not serve us. These are the learnt behaviours and patterns your Influencer has come to know.

When we honestly Self-Reflect by observing our thoughts and behaviours, we can recognise when we display our Influencer patterns. Once we know this, we can choose to act and react in ways that serve us. It is then that we create positive change in our lives. This is finding purpose.

Each time you learn and make changes this way, it breaks you away from your Influencer Self and moves you closer to aligning with your Authentic Self. Some examples that identify when you are operating from this definition of Life Purpose are: getting through the day without criticizing yourself; stopping smoking; practising better communication with your family; or accepting yourself and others more. So purpose isn't just one thing. It is found in everyday life as you are constantly faced with your Life Purpose Triangle. It is important to find purpose in everything that you do.

Building Blocks

People often describe a significant experience that has led them to find their purpose. While this may be, in part, true, it isn't the single event alone that caused their new-found understanding. The experience may have been the final block they used to complete the tower they were building. But if you were building a tower with blocks, you would first need a foundation; you would start with building your bottom layer, then move on to the middle and top sections, and finally put that final block on top.

Each time you have corrected your Influencer Self, you have learned more, evolved to your next development, and aligned closer with your Authentic Self. You were working towards building your tower through every change you made. You will always be evolving.

At times we may feel we have reached a point in our evolvement when we feel settled, but then find ourselves drained, tired, bored, fed up, and thinking to ourselves, 'How have I found myself at this place again?' But when we again reach the point of feeling unfulfilled or empty, it's because a part of our Influencer Selves is still living with us. So, when these feelings come up once more, it's not a bad thing. It's our Authentic Selves pushing us to relook at our Triangles in order to bring us back into alignment with our Authentic Selves.

Life Purpose is not a final destination. Because we will always evolve, we will continue to find purpose in new things.

Living Authentically

Our Authentic Self has so much magnificence that we cannot understand the amazing beings we are.

Your Authentic Self is the source of all your inner 'knowings', such as knowing right from wrong. It's the home of your intuition, your natural intellect, the unfiltered part of you, and your empathy, love, and Higher Power. The more you align with your Authentic Self, the more you discover your true purpose, which then offers you fulfilment. Once you align with your

Authentic Self, everything will feel right, and you will achieve fulfilment in everything you do.

Our interactions with one another, in the little things, allow us to live authentically. Each day we choose to react to someone not from hurt but from a state of understanding; we align with our Authentic Selves. The Authentic Self offers genuine kindness and pure love to others, whether we know them or not. It is that which, through any small action, leaves them feeling loved, cared for, and accepted.

Your Authentic Self is the part of you not governed by your habits, patterns, fears or your comfort zone and ego mind. It has a greatness unique to you, which no one else is born with, that is here to reach and connect with the people put on your path and to bring a specific teaching, love, and compassion that no one else can.

Once someone aligns with their Authentic Self, they no longer pretend to be someone they're not but are genuine in all their dealings and hold integrity within. Living life authentically and finding purpose gives people a sense of feeling alive, genuinely happy, free, content, and elated. The general feeling almost can't be described; it's almost like euphoria, a natural high that no drug or substitution could ever supply, yet feeling grounded at the same time. It's that feeling someone gets when they've acted on good intentions or have helped someone in need. This is the feeling that only the Authentic Self can provide. Living with purpose results in these feelings consistently.

Living in the Life Purpose Triangle means that your Authentic Self can wake up each morning not dreading the day but feeling alive and excited because the day ahead will have a purpose that provides fulfilment to you. All because you are doing what you are here to do.

Chapter 22
Become Your Own Miracle

Miracles. Some of us often pray for a miracle—some grand event that will change our lives in some extraordinary way. We look at what others have, and we want the same. We believe if we keep praying hard enough, someone or something will make them appear.

The irony is that you are already experiencing one miracle in your life right now, and that is YOU. We can achieve any of the miracles we want. All the prayers you need answered are within. Everything starts with you, yes, you have blessings in your life, like your family, your children and your close relationships with others, but the one who will help you achieve your own miracles is you. You can set intentions, send requests out to God and the Universe, and do all the manifesting your heart desires, but if you do not show that you truly want those things by putting in some effort, you will just be overruled by your Influencer.

There is absolutely nothing wrong with prayer. In fact, it can set good intentions, create, and help you vibrate on a higher level. The only problem with prayer is if you are physically waiting for what you pray for to fall onto your lap from some Higher Power.

You have the choice and the free will to give yourself everything. You are the higher power. Your Authentic Self is who will help deliver everything you need. Although, everything is just an idea if it's not lived. So why not start today? Start making your own miracles. Start living for you. Start by understanding the magnificence that you are.

I wish you love, patience, forgiveness, and understanding of your Life Purpose Triangle and leave you with a prayer.

> *Dear Me,*
>
> *I write and pray to you as we step into a path of self-discovery.*
>
> *Every day is a new adventure, excitement of the unknown;*
>
> *A path, a place where the unimaginable can happen.*
>
> *Let's believe, let's persevere, let's dream, let's share love, as this*
>
> *Is a place where all our dreams and desires exist.*
>
> *Let's open them one by one. Let's live out our true intention with*

love and integrity. It's all yours, waiting for you.

It's always been yours. Now you are ready. Now is the time.

Grab it with both hands.

—Love from your Authentic-Self

GLOSSARY

Your Story This is a series of connected events throughout your entire life. It is also the part of you where you believe you are the way you are because of your story.

Evolved Mental Maturity Your individual perception is unique to you. It consists of your beliefs and experiences—as you learn and change your behaviours, so does your Evolved Mental Maturity.

Evolvement Your evolvement is the process and steps you take each time you correct your actions, moving you closer to your Authentic Self.

Self-Identifying Labels These are thoughts you have about yourself, which have been projected onto you and suggested by others.

Conditioning This is the part of you that has developed because of the world you were born into, your home and early environment, and the area where you lived. It is where you were taught what to believe through culture, religion, and societal systems such as school, where you learnt personas, your learnt behaviours.

Influencer Self This is the part of you that has learnt all the things that do not serve you, your conditioning, habits, patterns, your self-identifying labels, where your comfort zone lives, all your man-made fears, where your ego lives, your negative self-worth and belief, this is the part of you that has made false associations to things, none of your Influencer Self is a true reality.

Observer Self The part of you that can view a situation and see what is really going on. This part can see from the outside in. It is almost like having an out-of-body experience where you are able to view yourself in action. It sees from a detached perspective.

Responsive Self This is the aspect of you that makes a decision only after your Observer is able to see what it is you are doing. It enables you to choose how to respond.

Authentic Self The part of you that is unique to you. It loves with great love. It does not hesitate to reach out to a stranger who collapses on the street. This is who you truly have always been before you learnt the things that do not serve you. As your inner being, who took human form, it knows your inner purpose and why you are here.

About the Author

Author Michelle Da Silva is the founder of SilvaVine and a professional life coach. She was born in Cape Town, South Africa. Her Portuguese parents moved to Cape Town, where she was raised until she was 18. She attended a girl's high school in Stellenbosch and helped work in her parent's fish and chips shop on the weekends. This helped her understand the importance of effort to achieve what you want.

After finishing school, she wanted to study law but decided to travel instead, moved to London, and had a successful career in catering.

Growing up, she was never drawn to writing. Only later in life did Michelle discover her interest in books. The only early hint of anything related to writing was her fascination with wanting a diary as a young girl. She never kept one as she was afraid someone might find and read it.

Michelle has experienced highs and lows in her life, like everyone else, but has always had a curiosity about life, the existence of all that is, the Universe, and everything in it. She always knew deep down that her aim was to work with people and help them reach their full potential, as this is what she wanted for herself.

Understanding Your Life Purpose Triangle was written to help as many people as possible. Michelle continues to help others via her talks, workshops, events, and one-to-one sessions. She lives in Surrey with her husband, Martin, and her two children, Ivy and Tyler.

Follow Michelle on her pages for events, exclusive offers and more.

⃝ @Silvavinecoaching

f Silvavine

www.ingramcontent.com/pod-product-compliance
Lightning Source LLC
Chambersburg PA
CBHW070426010526
44118CB00014B/1917